I0559512

STUFF KIDS SHOULD KNOW

How to Build Confidence, Overcome Challenges, Learn Financial Literacy, Set Goals, Master Resilience, Develop a Positive Mindset, and More!

JAKE RUSSELL

ISBN: 978-1-957590-39-4

For questions, email: Support@AwesomeReads.org

Please consider writing a review!

Just visit: AwesomeReads.org/review

FREE BONUS

SCAN TO GET OUR NEXT BOOK FOR FREE!

TABLE OF CONTENTS

INTRODUCTION

Wouldn't it be great if there was a manual on how to live the perfect life? You could just read that manual, follow the instructions, and your life would turn out exactly as you want. Well, that's not how life works, as you already know by now. However, there are skills and lessons that are a proven recipe for success in life, and that's what this book is all about.

1

We're not going to tell you how to live your life, and we're not going to hand you a magic formula that will make you rich and famous, but we can share some advice that has been shown to help people achieve the life they want—simply by being who they are. The earlier you learn this advice, the sooner you can start building the skills necessary to choose your path and become the kind of person you want to be.

Some people don't get the advice we're giving you until they're adults, which means they have a lot of learning to do and less time in which to learn it. Of course, the tips we provide are helpful at any age. You don't have to be a certain age to start using them, but if you can start learning these skills at a young age, you're way ahead of the game.

Structure

Each chapter will begin with an example of a well-known person who exemplifies the advice we're about to give. You'll see how these remarkable people used the skills in each chapter to accomplish their goals. Some of these people will be familiar to you, while others may be less so, but their brief stories will inspire you to learn more about how they applied important skills.

Following each story, we'll provide you with advice to help you achieve the overarching goals of the chapter. For example, Chapter 1 is about having a positive mindset, so we'll give you a few tips about how to manage negative thoughts and feelings.

At the end of each chapter, we'll give you a fun activity suggestion that allows you to practice the skills and advice from that section of the book. Remember, though, that doing the suggested activity is just a starting point. You'll still need to practice them often throughout your daily life.

Using the Advice

We want you to use the advice we give to improve yourself and open doors in your life that might otherwise be closed. However, that doesn't mean you should try to change everything at once. If you do that, you'll only grow frustrated and end up not making any lasting changes at all. Instead, talk with your parents or other trusted adults in your life about what they believe you should work on first. You might already know the answer they'll give, but it always helps to get an outside perspective so that you can focus on skills you *actually* need rather than the ones you think you need.

For example, you might think you know how to handle failure, so you don't need to read that section, but your mom feels differently. She remembers the last time you baked a cake and forgot to put enough eggs in the mixture. It was an honest mistake, but you got so frustrated that you refused to bake anything ever again. You gave up and let your failure override your love of baking and your dream of becoming a professional baker.

In this case, your mom would probably recommend you start working on handling failure, but as Chapter 11 will explain, if you truly believe you need a different skill even more, stand up for yourself and advocate for your own needs. As long as you do it kindly and respectfully, you'll be able to come to an agreement on how to use the advice we offer.

Making a Reading Plan

While some kids will read this book from beginning to end and then decide which skills they want to work on, others may know exactly which chapter they need right now and will read the book out of order. There's no right way or wrong way to read this book, but we recommend having a plan to ensure you read the entire thing. The advice and skills offered here work together to help you create the life you want. No single skill is more important than the other, so if reading the chapters out of order works for you, then by all means, make that your plan.

Another way to read the book is one chapter at a time. After you finish each chapter, do the suggested activity, then find ways to apply what you've learned to various situations in your life. This will be easier to do with some chapters because certain advice can be implemented right away. With others, you may have to wait until you find yourself in a situation where that advice comes into play before you'll be able to practice it.

No matter how you decide to read this book, consider reading it with a parent, sibling, or friend so that you can work on building the skills together and monitor each other's progress. Sometimes, it can be difficult to see if the advice is improving your own life, but you can clearly see how it's working in someone else's. Sharing this book with another person can only enhance its effectiveness as you practice roleplaying situations, put the advice into action, and hold feedback sessions to discuss progress with your partner. Often, it's easier to work on self-improvement when another person is doing it with you. That way, you can hold each other

4

accountable for practicing the advice, offer suggestions for improvement, and celebrate with them whenever you succeed.

One Last Note

Before we dive into the actual advice, we have one last note for you. The advice we're giving involves learning skills that you'll be practicing for a lifetime. You'll get better and better the more you use the advice, but even those who are considered masters at these skills still believe there's more they can learn.

This is just a starting point for you. Take this advice and run with it but continue finding ways to improve your skills to shape your life the way you want. Never be satisfied with where you are because there's always more you can do and become. Build on what you learn here to continually soar ever higher. When you're always striving to improve yourself and your life, the sky is truly the limit.

CHAPTER ONE: MINDSET MATTERS

A MAN NAMED NEIL

In 1969, Neil Armstrong became the first person to walk on the moon. This was an incredible accomplishment that no one had ever done before. Imagine how nervous Armstrong must have been! In fact, the astronaut himself said he was afraid of his moon mission failing.

Despite his fears, the Apollo 11 mission was a success, and Neil Armstrong went down in history. But what do you suppose would have happened if he'd let his fears get the better of him? He certainly would not have been the first man to walk on the moon. NASA might even have abandoned the Apollo 11 mission, and we wouldn't know half of what we do about our solar system. For example, missions to the moon were critical in studying how Earth came to be, the composition of the moon, and how important the moon is to our planet.

Before Apollo 11, no one had dared land on the moon, much less walk on it. In fact, no one was even sure it could be done. While people were excited, Armstrong included, there was also a lot of fear, especially of the unknown. This is always the case when you do something that has never been done before.

Despite those fears, Armstrong knew that many people were depending on him and the crew of Apollo 11. They had all prepared diligently and were ready to take advantage of the very unique opportunity before them. In fact, Armstrong said, "Success is where preparation meets opportunity. Work hard and prepare yourself because it's very difficult to predict what the future may bring, and you want to be ready when the opportunity of a lifetime comes your way." He knew they might never get the chance to land on the moon again, so instead of focusing on his fear, he kept a positive mindset and made history!

A positive mindset is one of the most powerful things you own. It will help you push through fear and uncertainty and encourage people around you to do the same. But how do you keep a positive mindset when all you can think about is the worst that could happen? The trick is learning to manage your negative thoughts and feelings. Think about Armstrong. He did have fears about the moon landing mission, but he didn't let them control him. When asked about the dangers he faced as commander of the Apollo 11 mission, Armstrong stated, "It's silly to say we don't think of the dangers. We do it all the time. But our job is to make those dangers less and less. I don't think of it as a personal danger."

Armstrong knew that dwelling on the danger would actually make the mission more dangerous because he would be second-guessing himself and possibly making mistakes that he wouldn't have made if he'd just relied on his training and preparation.

MANAGING NEGATIVE THOUGHTS AND FEELINGS

Step 1: Learn to Identify Negative Thoughts and Feelings

When you feel negative thoughts and feelings taking over, stop what you're doing and recognize that negativity by giving it a name: noise.

We call negative thoughts and feelings noise because, just like noise:

- Negative thoughts and feelings can be so loud that you can't hear anything else.
- Negative thoughts and feelings can feel overwhelming.
- Negative thoughts and feelings can make you feel very small.

Do you notice that all the feelings you get from listening to negative thoughts and feelings make you feel pretty lousy? No one likes to feel that way, but what can you do when the noise gets so loud that you can't hear anything else?

When something gets too noisy in life, we turn it down, which is what you should do to those negative thoughts and feelings. The next time you feel those negative thoughts and feelings getting too

10

noisy, imagine yourself turning down the volume just like you would for the television or radio.

_____

Question: What causes you to experience negative thoughts and feelings?

_____

Step 2: Think About What the Noise was Drowning Out

Now that you've turned down the noise ask yourself if there are any positive thoughts and feelings it was drowning out. Think about Neil Armstrong and how he turned down the volume on his noise and achieved so much by successfully completing the Apollo 11 mission. What could you achieve now that you've turned down the noise?

- Do you have a chance to do something life-changing?
- Could you learn something new?
- Will you be able to overcome your fear and enjoy a challenge?
- Could you help someone else?

When you turn down the noise, it's easier to notice other things, like how much you can grow as a person by being brave.

Question: Can you remember a time when you were able to listen to positive thoughts and feelings instead of negative ones?

Step 3: Compare Your Options

When you turn down the noise, you can see what else an experience has to offer. Now that you know your choices, you must decide: Do you turn the noise back up and listen to your fear and negative thoughts, or do you take charge and accept an opportunity to grow?

It is definitely easier to let negative thoughts and feelings tell you what to do, but that can leave you feeling like you have no control, or you're being held back by your fear.

Having a positive attitude and choosing to turn down the volume on those negative thoughts and feelings might be scary at first, but it can leave you feeling strong, brave, and accomplished.

Again, think about Neil Armstrong here. He could have chosen the less frightening option of not going to the moon, but he turned down the noise and chose the option of trying something new. His accomplishment speaks for itself as to how that choice turned out!

Question: How do you feel when you're able to overcome your negative thoughts and feelings?

Step 4: Realize That You're in Control

Nobody likes to feel like they don't have choices, and that's precisely what fear and negative thinking do: They take away your choice to try new things. However, if you can learn to identify sources of noise and turn down the volume on those negative thoughts and feelings, you can take control and decide what *you* want to do.

Remember, though, that choosing a positive attitude doesn't always mean saying yes to everything! Sometimes, you may decide not to do something simply because you do not want to, and that's okay. Just make sure you give yourself the option to make a choice without being pressured by a negative mindset and don't be discouraged if you have trouble thinking in a more positive way at first. Give yourself some grace, but don't give in. A positive attitude will not always come easily or naturally—even people like Neil Armstrong had to remind themselves to be brave sometimes!

TURNING DOWN THE VOLUME VS. IGNORING FEAR

Why do we turn down the volume on our fear? Why don't we ignore it instead? Well, because it isn't that simple.

Think of something you're afraid of doing, such as entering the school talent contest. What if someone says, "Just stop being afraid and enter the contest." Would that be very helpful? Do you think you could just stop being afraid because someone told you? Probably not. Your fear is real, even if it's something you can't explain; you can't just turn it off.

So, what good does turning down the noise of our fear do if it doesn't make it go away? Turning down the noise gives us a moment to think without being distracted. Our fear is still present, but turning down the volume lets us think with a cool head. For example, you might be afraid to enter a school talent competition because your fear says, "What if I don't win?" However, if you turn down the volume on that fear, you'll have a moment to think without that feeling of panic or defeat. You can ask yourself, "If I don't win, what's the worst that could happen?"

Most of the time, if you turn down your fear for long enough, you'll find that the things you're afraid of—the things that stop you from doing something—really aren't that scary at all.

Let us look at our example above. What's the worst that could happen if you enter the school talent competition?

- You might not win.
- You might feel embarrassed.
- You might feel discouraged.

Now, let's look at each situation and whether it's realistic and as bad as your fear says it is.

You might not win.

In most competitions, there can only be a handful of winners. It's possible that you could go home from the contest without winning, but you won't be the only one; most entrants in a competition won't win.

Will you be disappointed if you don't win? Of course! But is it the end of the world? Absolutely not. Just think of it as a rehearsal for many other future opportunities. Remember that life will offer you plenty of chances to succeed. This was just one of them.

You might feel embarrassed.

Sometimes, we put a lot of pressure on ourselves to be the best at everything. We tell ourselves that being anything less than the greatest is embarrassing or a failure. This is simply not true.

If, at the end of the day, you can sit back and say that you tried your best, there's nothing to be embarrassed about. You can only give 100 percent and expecting yourself (or others) to give more than that is unfair and unreasonable.

You might feel discouraged.

It can feel very discouraging to try your best but not get the result you want. Here's the thing no one tells you, though: Everyone feels that way sometimes. When that happens, it can be tempting to sit back and wallow in your feelings but ask yourself what good can come from feeling negative. Instead of getting discouraged, be proud of yourself for trying something you were afraid to do and use that as motivation to keep trying.

Now that you've had a moment to think without being bullied by fear ask yourself, "Are the things I'm afraid of happening that terrible, or is my fear making me think the worst?" Sometimes, all you need to do is turn down the volume on your fear to see things a little more clearly.

Have a Growth Mindset to Improve Yourself

Having a positive mindset is often enough to power yourself through many challenges that you'll encounter in your life, but you might need a little more help sometimes. This is where having a growth mindset comes into the picture. A growth mindset is basically the belief that most skills and abilities can be developed through persistence and hard work. In other words, if you keep trying to succeed at something, you'll eventually do it.

A growth mindset is the opposite of a fixed mindset, which is when people believe they're born with certain talents and abilities, and

16

they aren't able to acquire additional ones. For example, some people believe they're bad at math and always will be. That's a fixed mindset. However, having a growth mindset means they believe they can get better if they keep practicing. People with a growth mindset don't give up when it gets hard. Instead, they continue to practice and build their skills until they succeed. This doesn't mean they won't stumble on other math concepts in the future, but it does mean they can overcome the challenges they encounter if they keep working toward that goal.

Having a growth mindset is part of having a positive mindset because you refuse to let your mistakes and failures prevent you from reaching your goals. Instead, you reframe those mistakes and failures as learning opportunities. You use what you learned from them to try new ways to succeed. In other words, you view your challenges as trial and error until you find the right solution.

Let's look at an example. Pretend you want to open a lemonade stand. You get your supplies, choose a corner, and set up shop, but no one comes. At the end of the day, you haven't made a dime. Someone with a fixed mindset might say, "Well, I'm not a businessperson. I don't have what it takes to open even a lemonade stand, much less become an entrepreneur when I get older." A person with a growth mindset might say, "I wonder what I could do differently to succeed." Then they might look at things like location, weather, price, and advertising as factors they could change about their lemonade stand to get customers to buy their product. They might change one part of their business at a time to see what works until they get the outcome they desire.

So, in the case of the lemonade stand, one failure doesn't mean you aren't cut out for business or that you can't be an entrepreneur. It just means that you need to try something different to see if it works, and if it doesn't, try again. You're learning new things every time you try something else, and those new skills will eventually work together for a successful outcome. What's even better is that you'll have skills that can be used to conquer other challenges in the future.

Fun activity suggestion: Draw a picture of yourself being positive and happy.

CHAPTER TWO: BUILDING SELF-CONFIDENCE

A MAN NAMED THOMAS

In 1847, the Edison family welcomed their seventh child, a boy named Thomas. By the time Thomas was 12 years old, he had lost hearing in one ear and had very poor hearing in the other (although historians can't quite agree on how this happened). In the same year, Thomas Edison left school to work on the railroad.

During the Civil War, Edison set about learning more about the new telegraph technology that allowed people who were physically far apart to quickly send complicated messages. Although he picked up the technology immediately, the telegraph industry soon introduced sound, putting him at a disadvantage in the field because of his poor hearing. Edison was intrigued by the telegraph technology, but his disadvantage concerned him, so he began to invent gadgets that would help him compensate for his deafness. By 1969, Edison quit his job to dedicate all his time to inventing.

By the time he died in 1931, Edison held 1,093 invention patents, including designs for the incandescent light bulb, the phonograph, the movie camera, and the modern electrical system. Edison didn't give up working with a technology that he loved because of poor accessibility. Instead, he turned to a life of invention—one that would eventually lead him to create some of today's most critical technologies! But what do you suppose would have happened if Edison had accepted society excluding him because of his hearing? If he hadn't contributed to the world in the way he did, we would certainly be decades behind in technological advances, and many industries wouldn't be where they are today.

A strong sense of self-confidence plays a crucial role in your success as a human being, but how do you begin to build your self-confidence? The trick is learning to accept yourself for who you are, much like Thomas Edison did.

LOVING AND ACCEPTING YOURSELF

One of the most important things you can do to build your self-confidence is to love yourself for who you are. When you're confident in yourself, people see that confidence the moment you walk into a room. People want to get to know you. They want to feel as confident as you do. They want to bask in the company of someone who is comfortable with who they are.

And here's the funny thing: You don't even have to feel confident at first! Have you ever heard someone say, "Fake it until you make it"? The longer you pretend to have confidence in yourself, the easier it becomes to truly feel that way. No one but you can tell the difference between faking it and "making it."

But how do you start to fake it?

Every morning when you wake up, before you even get out of bed, come up with five things that you love about yourself. Do the same thing every day, whether you feel loving toward yourself or not.

21

Over time, as you start the day off on a confident note, it will get easier and easier to continue doing it, and you'll find that it makes you feel pretty good!

There are so many people picking apart our lives, pointing out what's wrong with us, and shining a light on our flaws that it's no surprise we fall into a slump. If you constantly tell yourself that you can't do something or you aren't what you should be, then you'll start to believe it. The key to a happy life is doing the exact opposite. Train your brain to focus on the good things. Love who you are.

Now, remember that being confident and loving yourself isn't the same as thinking you don't have faults. Everyone has faults. Being confident means owning those faults and doing what you can to improve on them while also recognizing the things that you cannot change.

TRY NEW THINGS AND TAKE RISKS

Accepting yourself for who you are does wonders for your self-confidence, and having more self-confidence makes it easier to try new things and take risks that you might not have taken before. This can be scary because the human brain likes routine and knowing what to expect; it resists change and the unknown. Getting out of your comfort zone signals "danger" to your brain, but if you're not actually putting yourself in physical danger, doing new things is critical to personal development.

Why is it important to try new things and take risks? Why can't you just sit back and be comfortable in your newfound self-confidence? To grow as a person, you must expand your horizons, and that means exposing your brain to different experiences so that it can create new pathways and connections. Besides that, trying new things and taking risks can lead you to discover amazing things!

For example, if you really like chocolate, try to think about a time when you'd never tasted it. Imagine if you'd been afraid to try something new and you decided that you didn't want to try chocolate. You would have missed out on all these years of deliciousness.

Now, not everything that you decide to take a chance on is going to turn out like chocolate. Sometimes, you might do something new and decide that it really isn't right for you, and that's okay too. Finding out what we don't like is just as important as finding out what we do.

Just because you're pushing yourself to try new things doesn't mean that you must say yes to every opportunity. Use your common sense. Some new experiences really are physically dangerous, and your brain is telling you to avoid them for a reason.

For example, if a friend invites you to go bungee jumping, you might be afraid but decide that you would like to try it anyway just to say you did! On the other hand, if a friend tells you to drive their car home even though you don't have your license, your common sense should tell you that it's not the time to take a risk.

Taking risks can help us to grow as people, but we still have to use our brains to consider consequences before making decisions. If the risks are too big, or if the risks outweigh the rewards, that little voice inside your head should remind you to politely pass on the activity. Never stop listening to that little voice.

TAKE CARE OF YOURSELF

While we're talking about listening to that little voice inside your head, the last thing to remember when building your self-confidence is to take care of yourself. Often, when we think about taking care of ourselves, we think about going to the gym or eating well, but that isn't all there is to self-care. Proper self-care involves taking good physical care of yourself, taking good psychological care of yourself, and making good decisions.

Physical Fitness

While physical fitness isn't everything, it's still important. The healthier you feel, the easier it is to stay positive about life and make good choices. If you neglect your physical fitness, you may start to feel physically limited and even depressed. These feelings can quickly take over and reverse all the positive changes you've been trying to make.

Staying on top of your physical fitness isn't just about being super athletic or a member of the varsity team; there are many things you can do to achieve and maintain physical fitness.

- Take part in a sport by joining a school athletic team or an after-school community team.
- Play physical games like basketball with friends.
- Walk or ride your bike.
- Practice yoga as a gentle form of exercise.
- Do light stretches first thing in the morning.
- Instead of asking someone else to get something for you, get up and get it yourself.

Anything that gets your heart rate up just a little bit can help keep you healthier and happier. Staying in good physical shape can also boost your self-esteem and contribute to a genuine feeling of self-confidence.

Psychological Fitness

Just as it's important to keep your body in good physical shape, it is important to keep your mind in good shape, too. Keeping your mind in good shape might seem a little more difficult to do than keeping your body in good shape, but it's actually fairly easy!

Psychological fitness centers around balance. This means making time for work and play. For example, go to school and do your homework, but also give yourself time to decompress by doing things you like to do for fun, like playing video games and reading books. Remember that it's also important to be mindful of how much time you spend doing any activity. It may sound funny, but just like your psychological health can be thrown off by doing too much work, it can be thrown off by doing too much of something like playing video games!

Making Good Decisions

Another part of taking care of yourself is making good decisions. When you have confidence in your ability to make good decisions, you experience much less stress throughout your life. Don't confuse making good decisions with making safe decisions, though. Just as we mentioned before, you should challenge yourself to take risks and try new things, but don't let that desire lead you to make an unsafe decision.

But how do you learn to make good and safe decisions?

A lot of times, you can make the right decision just by listening to your gut (or that voice in the back of your head that tells you when something is a really bad idea). For example, if a friend asks you to do something that you know you shouldn't, you might get a feeling in the pit of your stomach or hear that voice in your head telling you not to do it. Learn to listen to those things; they're your body's way of telling you that whatever you're thinking about doing is a bad idea.

Other times, you may not have the instinct that something isn't safe because you haven't fully developed your decision-making skills yet. In cases where you're not sure if you should do something or not, ask an adult. Your brain is still growing, and you might need some help to recognize the risks involved with certain things. Making mistakes is part of life, and if the situation truly isn't dangerous, the adult will allow you to try it and make the mistake so that you can learn from it. Their lifelong experience gives them an advantage over your limited knowledge, and their advice can keep you from doing something that could be life-altering.

So how do you know when something is a good idea? You might be excited about it, or you might be a little bit nervous, but you won't hear that voice or feel that funny feeling in the pit of your stomach. You also may need to talk to an adult to make sure it's a good idea or not. Again—as a kid, your brain hasn't fully developed its decision-making abilities yet, and we can all use a little help sometimes when it comes to making hard choices.

It's important to remember that making good decisions is also a learning process; at times, you might think that you're making a good decision when you're not. Just remember that everyone makes bad decisions sometimes. As long as you learn from the bad mistakes that you do make, you can walk away from them a wiser person.

Fun activity suggestion: Write down things you love about yourself on sticky notes and put them on your mirror.

27

CHAPTER THREE: THE ART OF COMMUNICATION

A MAN NAMED GEORGE

There's an old saying: "Fool me once, shame on you; fool me twice, shame on me." In September 2002, a man named George got himself tied in knots as he tried to remember it correctly. The resulting speech went like this: "There's an old saying in Tennessee—I know it's in Texas, probably in Tennessee—that says, fool me once, shame on—shame on you. Fool me—you can't get fooled again." The George who made this blunder was President George W. Bush. This wasn't the only time that the president goofed when he spoke. In fact, President George W. Bush became known for his "Bushisms."

For the average person to make this kind of mistake, it might be no big deal, but for a man who is responsible for running the entire country, it raised questions. After all, people expect the president to be intelligent and well-spoken. Making a few verbal blunders doesn't mean you lack intelligence; it just means you made some mistakes. However, those errors can affect the way people view you, even if that's not fair.

Effective communication is only possible when you can efficiently express yourself and actively listen to others. Once you've mastered these communication skills, a new world of possibilities opens up. But how do you begin to develop your communication skills?

EXPRESS YOURSELF EFFECTIVELY

Being able to express yourself effectively requires clear communication skills, excellent listening skills, and compassion. With the perfect combination of these factors, you can:

- be a better friend.
- be more clearly understood.
- avoid confrontation.
- become a better public speaker.
- build lifelong friendships.
- open yourself up to new possibilities.
- advance your career.

The first step in developing these good communication skills is learning how to express yourself effectively and think ahead.

Think First

Have you ever started to say something without thinking first? You wind up talking gibberish because all the words try to come out at once, or you can't quite think of the right words, so you stop mid-sentence. This happens when you don't think before you speak.

Expressing yourself effectively starts with knowing what you want to say before you try to say it. The next time you have something to say, if you don't have time to write it down and practice it, take a few moments to go over what you want to say in your head. A quiet rehearsal in your head lets you straighten out your thoughts and make sure that what you're about to say makes sense.

Assess What You're About to Say

Stopping to think before you speak is good practice for expressing yourself effectively, *and* it gives you time to assess whether you should say what you're thinking. Have you ever heard someone say that you should think before you speak? The reason that people say this is because sometimes you say things that you don't mean if you don't think about the impact of your words. For example, you might be angry right now and say hurtful things to someone that you regret saying later.

You can avoid saying things that you might regret by asking yourself a few questions when you stop to think. Use the acronym THINK to decide whether what you're about to say is:

- True
- Helpful
- Inspiring
- Necessary
- Kind

If you answer no to any of those, take another minute to rethink what you were about to say, or don't say anything at all. Many arguments can be avoided by simply not saying things you think, but to avoid this, you have to really think first so that the words don't accidentally come out of your mouth.

32

Enunciate

Expressing yourself effectively isn't only about planning. It's also about enunciating or speaking clearly and pronouncing words properly. Knowing what you want to say or saying the right thing won't matter if you don't speak clearly because people still won't understand you. Mumbling, speaking too softly, or not clearly enunciating your words can lead to all sorts of misunderstandings.

If people often misunderstand you when you speak, try speaking slower and really pronouncing the words you want to say. Make sure people can hear each word you say. Practice is also key to developing the skill of enunciation. We often mumble words if we're unsure of how to pronounce them in hopes that our audience won't notice. This doesn't work very often, though. People are drawn to the mumbled words and become more focused on the mistake than they would be otherwise.

It's always better to practice speeches if you have time so that you can learn the pronunciation of any unfamiliar words before you speak in front of a live audience. You'll also find out if you speak too fast for people to follow you or if you need to speak louder so that they can hear you. All these factors affect your enunciation. One good idea is to record yourself as you speak so that you can determine for yourself where you might need to improve.

Be Concise

While we're on the topic of each word that you say, the last thing to keep in mind when learning to express yourself effectively is to be concise. Has someone ever started telling you about something that happened but taken far too long or get distracted? By the time they finish their story, you're just hoping they'll stop talking. Once you're thinking about that, you're not paying attention to what the person is saying. To prevent this, you should always be concise with what you have to say. In other words, get to the point!

The next time you have a story to tell, try to avoid extra details that aren't important to your story and make sure you don't get distracted and go off on unrelated tangents while you're talking.

LISTEN TO OTHERS

Knowing how to express yourself effectively is about more than getting other people to understand you. It's also about listening. For example, if you listen when your boss tells you that she rewards employees who show initiative, you can show her how dedicated you are by finding new tasks whenever you aren't busy. This lets your boss know that you pay attention to details and that you appreciate your job.

Listening well also helps you communicate more effectively because it means that you're educated on the topic you're talking about. It also lets people know you're paying attention to them.

But what makes you a *good* listener?

Being Present

Do you ever find your mind wandering when someone else is talking? When you aren't paying attention, you can miss important information, offend the person speaking, and make yourself look disrespectful.

Instead of letting your mind wander when someone else is talking, try to be consciously present. Let the person in front of you know that you're listening by focusing on them and not getting distracted.

Actively Listening

Active listening is more than just listening to someone. It means listening and investing yourself in what they're saying. For example, if a friend tells you they just had a fight with another friend, instead of just listening to them talk, you might ask them what the fight was about or how they felt about it. These questions show that you're giving your friend your full attention and that what they're saying is important to you.

When you are actively listening to someone, be sure to pay attention and give pertinent feedback. Don't just ask generic questions to make it seem as though you're listening. Nine times out of ten, the person who's talking will know that you're faking interest.

Don't Interrupt

Interrupting someone when they're talking is rude because you're telling them that what they're saying isn't important or interesting to you. Interrupting also makes you look like a jerk because you think that what you have to say is more important. If you have something to say when someone else is talking, wait until they've finished and then share your thoughts.

EMPATHY AND KINDNESS

Communicating clearly and being a good listener are key factors in efficient communication, but you also need to be able to put yourself in someone else's shoes. This means being able to experience something from their point of view. You can do this by asking yourself how you would feel if you were in their situation. For example, if one of your parents isn't feeling well and you're playing video games loudly with your friend, you might feel angry if they ask you to be quiet. If your first instinct is to feel angry, take a moment to think about how your parent feels. Can you remember a time when you were ill? How did you feel? Now, how would you have felt if someone had been making a lot of noise when you felt that way? What can you do to be kind? In this example, you might remember how rotten you felt when you had the flu and stop making a noise or even offer to make your parent something to eat or drink.

Sometimes, we can get so caught up in ourselves that we forget to think about other people. It only takes a few seconds to stop and remind yourself to think about someone else and do something kind instead of selfish. Being able to put yourself in someone else's shoes makes a huge difference in how people treat you. You might also be surprised to know that when you're able to put yourself in someone else's shoes, you tend to feel better about yourself too!

PUTTING IT ALL TOGETHER

As you can see, expressing yourself efficiently is about being able to communicate well with others in more ways than one. By getting your point across clearly, listening to others, and showing them compassion, your interactions with other people have much more meaning. You will also find that you develop stronger bonds with people, create new friendships, strengthen relationships, and open many new possibilities for yourself and your future!

Let's quickly recap how each of these skills can be beneficial to you now and in the future.

- Thinking before you speak ensures you say what you mean to avoid misunderstandings that could impact your relationships with others and your future work opportunities.
- Assessing what you're about to say ensures you won't say something you might regret, costing yourself friendships or even your job.
- Enunciating makes sure that you aren't misunderstood when speaking, something that can cause embarrassing mistakes.
- Being concise helps keep other people's interest, and it's a great skill to have for any future employment opportunity.

- Actively listening allows you to stay informed about situations and avoid careless mistakes or misunderstandings.
- Not interrupting makes other people feel like what they have to say is important and encourages them not to interrupt you when you're speaking.
- Putting yourself in other people's shoes gives you a more well-rounded view of the world and makes you more relatable.

If President George W. Bush had rehearsed what he was going to say and taken his time to say it, he wouldn't have made his blunder in September 2002—a blunder that is so well known, it's even sampled in a popular song by J. Cole!

Fun activity suggestion: Play a game where you take turns telling a story and listening to each other.

CHAPTER FOUR: MAKING AND KEEPING FRIENDS

TWO MEN NAMED HENRY AND THOMAS

When we talked about building self-confidence, we talked about a man named Thomas Edison. Did you know that Thomas Edison had a very good friend named Henry? In 1891, Henry Ford went to work for the Edison Illuminating Company, and in 1896, he met Thomas Edison at the Association of Edison Illuminating Companies conference. Ever since he was a boy, Henry idolized Thomas Edison, and when he finally had a chance to meet him, it changed his life forever.

At the time of their meeting, Ford had just built a quadricycle, and Edison encouraged him to keep working on his invention as he believed that the future was in electric cars. Ford continued to pursue his work, and the two inventors forged a strong friendship. Ford even invested in Edison's car battery project. The two inventors were such lifelong friends that they became neighbors and, in their old age, raced against each other in their wheelchairs.

Without their friendship, who knows whether Ford would have invented the automobile as we know it. It's possible that Edison would never have raised the money he needed to develop the car battery further.

Humans are a social species, and whether we like it or not, we need each other to survive. We live close to each other, we go to school together, and we play together. This social nature means that we need companionship and interaction with others to thrive and be

40

happy. Having friends is about more than social interaction and happiness, though; friends also provide us with encouragement and a social support network that's crucial to developing social skills.

But how do you go about making and keeping friends? The trick is learning to be accepting of others, always being willing to compromise, and having fully open lines of communication.

BUILDING AND MAINTAINING FRIENDSHIPS

As children, friendships can come quite easily; making friends is as simple as having similar interests or sharing snacks at lunch. Some people are fortunate enough to carry those friendships with them through the rest of their lives.

Maintaining Friendships

Maintaining friendships can be difficult. Having lifelong friendships means that you have friends who have been through life's highs and lows with you. These friends know you, and the bond that you have means that you can trust them to help you make major decisions in your life.

You may be wondering how to maintain friendships, especially when your life is getting more chaotic as you grow older. Try to remember that both you and your friends are growing up. You all face new challenges that force you to change your lives but remind

41

yourself to check in with your friends now and then. Provide a listening ear, ask how they're doing, offer advice if it is asked of you, and take a couple of hours each week to do something fun together to unwind. An hour or two really isn't that much time out of your weekly schedule, and you'll both benefit from sharing that time together.

Sometimes, giving up a couple of hours each week might seem like a chore, but by spending time together, you make sure that your friendship doesn't just become a relationship where you call on each other in times of need. Friendships that become about nothing but doing favors and helping each other out quickly start to decay.

The bottom line is that you must refill the cup of friendship rather than drain it all the time. If all you do is drain it, there will come a time when there's nothing left.

Making New Friends

Some people spend most of their lives with one group of friends, while others experience life changes that result in moving away from old friends. Even though it's important to keep in touch with those old friends, you should also work on building new friendships too so that you have a support network locally.

Building new friendships can be difficult, particularly as you get older. If you don't belong to any clubs or sports at school, it might be challenging to find other people with the same interests. This is especially true when you outgrow your current school and move to the next level. Since your routine is entirely different, you might not feel confident enough to step forward and make new friends.

42

Even though these situations can feel uncomfortable, it's always best to remind yourself that you have nothing to lose and give it a shot anyway. If you don't make an effort to build a friendship, you may just be missing out on the best friend you ever had.

Be Inclusive and Accepting of Others

One of the best ways to make friends is to be inclusive and accepting of others. Just as you would like people to accept you for who you are, you must also make an effort to accept others as they are. You never know what you might learn from someone, even if they seem like they're different from you. Remember that everyone who comes into your life has the potential to teach you something, so why not find out what that something is by giving yourself a chance to get to know them?

Being inclusive of others doesn't just open you up to more friendships; it makes an impact on the other people around you. By being accepting, you can teach others to be accepting too.

But what does it mean to be inclusive and accepting of others?

INCLUSIVITY

Being inclusive of others means making everyone feel included and welcome.

Have you ever been the new person to a group of friends? Did you feel accepted or like an outsider? Did those friends include you in their conversations, or did they share inside jokes that left you feeling confused? If those friends were being inclusive, they would include you in their conversations and make a conscious effort not to talk about things that made you feel like you weren't part of the group. For example, a group of friends might ask you questions about the things that you like or talk about experiences that you share.

Being inclusive isn't only important in new friendships. Everyone should strive to be inclusive every day of their life, from childhood through adulthood.

Some ways that you can try to be more inclusive include:

- Not making assumptions
- Educating yourself
- Listening fully
- Asking questions
- Thinking before you speak

One of the most important things you can do to be inclusive of others is to accept them.

BEING ACCEPTING OF OTHERS

Being accepting of others means recognizing a person for who they are and understanding that they have the right to be their own person. This includes understanding that everyone has their own feelings and opinions. You don't have to share the same opinions

44

or have the same feelings as someone else, but you should always be tolerant and empathetic.

Accepting other people isn't always easy. We would all like to think we're welcoming of everyone, or we always make the right choices, but the truth is that we don't. For example, there might be someone in your class who has a different religious belief than you. When you hear about the holy days that they celebrate or the different requirements their religion has, you might find it strange. You may find it difficult to connect with this person because that part of their life is so different from your own.

Most people are a little unsure when they meet someone different from themselves because they don't know how to relate. But what makes you a better person — someone who accepts others — is what you do with that uncertainty. Do you avoid that person? Do you laugh when someone makes a joke about their religion? Or do you try harder to do better? It takes work to realize that you simply don't understand that part of that person's life and make a conscious choice to educate yourself. The only way to overcome feeling unsure about others is to put in the effort to understand those differences. When you try to understand the things that make others different, you take away the uncertainty and give yourself a chance to find common ground. This also makes you into a better person.

In the example above, you might try learning about that person's religion. If you have questions about something, respectfully ask them. For example, you might say, "I heard you say something about Eid, and I was wondering if you might tell me a bit more about it." This lets the other person know that you're interested in learning more about them. It's a way to show you're not trying to change them, and you won't make fun of them for being different. Most importantly, it lets them know that you're an accepting person and someone they can feel safe around.

Talk to Your Friends and Work Out Problems

What if your friends aren't as accepting of others? What if you make an effort to get to know someone who's different, but your friends just make fun of that person? When this type of situation happens, you have two choices: You can say something, or you can say nothing. Which would you do? If you say nothing, it means that you're condoning their behavior or approving of what they're doing even though it hurts someone else or makes that person feel unsafe. If you say something, you risk your friends disagreeing with you.

Having friends disagree can be upsetting, but it's more important to be able to do the right thing. In this situation, you should speak up for the other person. Remind your friends that they all have things about themselves that are different too. Let your friends know that you care about their friendship but don't like the choices that they've made; explain why it's important that they try harder to do better.

Just because all your friends feel a certain way doesn't mean that you have to feel that way too. Making the right choice is always a better option than making the easy choice. If you try talking to your friends, they might realize they were in the wrong. If your friends still refuse to accept another person's differences, then you might need to reevaluate your friendships.

Yes, friendships are valuable and important throughout your lifetime, but only healthy friendships allow you to live and grow. True friends will work out differences. True friends will figure out a way to work past differences and be respectful of each other. If a friend is not a true friend, then ask yourself if you can afford to have them in your life.

What does it mean to afford a friend? When you have a friend, you give part of yourself to them. You support your friends, give affection to them, and share your time with them. In return, a true friend does the same for you. If someone isn't a true friend and they stress you out, you wind up giving more of yourself and receiving nothing in return. This type of friendship isn't just unfair; it's also emotionally draining and unhealthy for you.

Fun activity suggestion: Plan a fun activity with friends and try to include everyone.

CHAPTER FIVE: COPING WITH FAILURE AND DISAPPOINTMENT

A MAN NAMED HARLAND

In 1930, a man named Harland turned 40 years old and started selling chicken at a restaurant and motel. Over the years, he worked to perfect his cooking technique and his secret fried chicken recipe. His food became increasingly popular. Eventually, a new highway was built that took drivers away from Harland's restaurant, and he was forced to sell at the age of 65 and retire.

Harland wasn't ready to settle down, though, and he decided to take what little money he had left and hit the road to sell his chicken recipe. He visited restaurants and even cooked his recipe up for restaurant owners to show them how delicious his recipe was. Do you know that Harland was turned down 1,009 different times before he finally had a restaurant accept his offer? Despite being turned down over 1,000 times and being an old man, Harland persevered because he knew that he had something worth selling. Most of us now know him as Colonel Harland Sanders, or Colonel Sanders for short.

Setbacks and failures are a part of life, and how well you handle them tells a lot about who you are and how resilient and resourceful you can be. You can use failure as an opportunity to grow or let it get the best of you, but only one of those will help you become a better person. The trick to coping with failures and disappointments is always to learn from them, even if the failures weren't yours!

HANDLING SETBACKS AND FAILURES

Everyone experiences setbacks and failures at some point in their life, but what distinguishes you is how you deal with them. Imagine being Colonel Sanders. Would you have handled his situation the same way he did? Would you have kept trying until you got the result you wanted? When you're faced with obstacles in your path, you have two choices: You can give up, or you can find a way around the obstacle. For example, Colonel Sanders wanted to sell his chicken recipe, but every time someone said no to buying it, it created another obstacle for him. But Colonel Sanders used every no as motivation to keep going. If he hadn't, there's a good chance you would never know what Kentucky Fried Chicken tastes like!

Do you feel defeated when you hit a lot of obstacles in your path? Most of us do. But if you really want something, you have to work hard for it, and you can't let obstacles stand in your way. For example, is there a job you really want to do when you get older? What if someone told you that you can't do that job unless you first take a college course? Would you do it? Imagine that once you take the course and think you're ready to start the job you've always wanted, someone else says there's another requirement. How many obstacles would you overcome before you gave up on your dream career?

BE RESILIENT AND NEVER GIVE UP

If you ever feel like giving up, ask yourself this: What would you gain from giving up? In the example above, you've already taken one course. You've invested your time and your money into getting your dream job. Do you really want to give up now? If you do, you won't have anything to show for your efforts but lost time and money. But if you keep your sights on the finish line and push forward, you can cross it.

Sometimes, obstacles to our success can be more than having to take a class. They can be serious or even devastating. These types of obstacles can be much more difficult to overcome, but if you are resilient and never give up, you can still come out on top.

But how do you stay motivated, particularly during those really difficult times?

Review Your Progress

When you experience setbacks and obstacles, it can help to look back at your progress so far. What have you already accomplished? Even small steps are steps toward your goal, and regularly reviewing those small steps can help keep you going!

Stay Positive

When you feel like you're losing motivation, staying positive can convince you to keep pushing forward. If you have trouble staying positive yourself, surround yourself with positive people. Just being in the company of other people who are positive can help change your mindset.

Remind Yourself of Your Goals

Sometimes, we can get so consumed by the obstacles we're trying to overcome that we forget about why we're facing them in the first place. Stopping once in a while to remind yourself of your goals can give you a little boost to keep going.

If you still feel disheartened when you remind yourself of your goals, try making some smaller milestones. Smaller goals give you something easier to achieve so that you can feel a sense of accomplishment more frequently.

Take a Break

At times, obstacles can feel so insurmountable that you need to take a break, step back, and give yourself some grace. Remind yourself that you don't have to overcome that obstacle today. Remind yourself that you're human. Take a little time to regroup and re-energize. After a break, you may find that you can look at the situation with renewed energy.

Learn From Mistakes

When you pursue your goals, you might make mistakes. For example, you might make the mistake of not researching a potential career, so you were unaware of the classes you might need to take. When you make a mistake, you might be tempted to feel like a failure, or like you've wasted time. Instead of beating yourself up, learn what you can and use that to make better decisions later. So, in the above example, you might learn how important it is to be thorough in your research, which is a lesson that you can apply in the future. So yes, you may have made a mistake, but if you learned something from that mistake, then it's not wasted time.

Do you know that sometimes at job interviews, you will be asked about mistakes you've made and what you learned from them? This is because employers want to hire someone who acknowledges that they make mistakes and learns from them. We're all human, and everyone makes mistakes. What you do with the information that you learn from your mistakes is what matters.

Fun activity suggestion: Play a game where you turn a mistake into something positive.

CHAPTER SIX: RESPONSIBILITY AND ACCOUNTABILITY

A MAN NAMED JOHN

In 1961, America and the Soviet Union (USSR) were in conflict over whose nation was the strongest superpower, and the dictator Fidel Castro ruled Cuba. The U.S. Government didn't care for Castro and how he treated his people, and they refused to trade with Cuba. This trade ban upset the Cuban dictator, so he took control of American properties in Cuba and allied himself with the Soviet Union.

When Cuba allied with the USSR, President John F. Kennedy decided it was time for America to show Russia and Cuba that America meant business. Kennedy pushed forward plans to invade Cuba to try and get rid of Fidel Castro in an attack called the Bay of Pigs Invasion. Unfortunately, Cuba was much more prepared than expected, and the attack failed miserably and caused many casualties. When the attack failed, Kennedy admitted his fault and took responsibility for the failure because he was the "responsible officer of the Government."

After this speech, President Kennedy's approval ratings among the American people skyrocketed. The American people appreciated his honesty and that he held himself responsible for his own actions.

Responsibility and reliability are critical qualities; they are valuable to employers, friends, and family and should matter to you too. By proving your reliability, you not only show that you're

56

someone who's trustworthy, but you also show that you understand the consequences of your actions. But how do you begin to become more responsible and accountable?

The trick to responsibility and accountability is holding yourself responsible for your actions and learning to own up to your mistakes.

BE RESPONSIBLE FOR YOUR ACTIONS

One of the most important lessons that you'll learn as an adult is the value of being responsible for your actions. Let's face it: No one likes being wrong. If we could be right all the time, we wouldn't have to worry about negative consequences. However, we're all human, which means we're not right all the time. But, like John F. Kennedy, if we admit we were wrong and try to fix it, we often gain a lot more respect and admiration from other people.

It's far easier to blame other people or situations for our actions because it makes us feel better about ourselves. However, in the long run, we only cheat ourselves by not owning our actions and our part in a mistake or failure. When our actions cause negative consequences for ourselves or others, and we don't take responsibility, we don't learn from them, and we're almost guaranteed to make similar mistakes in the future.

There's a saying that the universe will keep giving you the same challenge in different ways until you learn how to overcome it. If you never take responsibility for failing that challenge, you're going to keep encountering it one way or another until you do. It's not really the universe working against you, though. It has more to do with having a growth mindset. Once you develop the necessary skills to succeed, you'll already know how to overcome the challenge the next time you see it, so it won't look like a true obstacle anymore.

Taking responsibility for your actions also helps keep your relationships with other people strong and healthy. They will know that you're a person of your word and that they can trust you to do the right thing, even if it means admitting you were wrong, to begin with. They know you won't place the blame on them or anything else, which is frequently the reason relationships fail.

Think about someone in your life who made a mistake and blamed someone else. How do you feel about that person now? Even if that person is someone very close to you, it's possible that you don't trust them as much as you used to. That's a natural reaction because we want to distance ourselves from people who might blame us when something goes wrong.

It's far better to take responsibility for your actions from the beginning so that you don't spend time worrying about whose fault the failure was. Instead, you're focused on changing the way you approach the issue and getting the outcome you want. Playing the blame game is wasted energy—energy that could be spent finding a solution.

This doesn't mean you should take responsibility for others' actions just to move things along to the solution phase. That doesn't help the person who actually made the mistakes. You'll learn more about this later in Chapter 11, but for now, know that you don't have to and shouldn't take the blame for something you didn't do just to keep the peace.

Here's how to own up to your mistakes so that they can be learning tools instead of something you dread:

Step 1:

If you recognize the mistake, it's better to acknowledge it right away than to wait for someone else to find the mistake and bring it up. This way, you can get out in front of it and come up with possible solutions first. Take a good look at the mistake and think about how you can fix it. Sometimes, you don't even have to get anyone else involved. You can just apply your solution and move on.

If you do need to get someone else involved, coming to them with possible solutions will show that you acknowledge the mistake and want to do what you can to make it right. It doesn't mean you won't have consequences, but they will be limited to the damage already done instead of continuing damage that could occur by not admitting your mistake.

Step 2:

Keep your mistake in perspective. Even if you're embarrassed about making the mistake, it's probably not the end of the world.

59

You might feel like it is for a while, but in the bigger picture, it's mostly likely fairly minor. Your embarrassment will pass, leaving you a stronger and more resilient person because you faced the situation head-on.

Step 3:

Be honest and take responsibility. Explain the mistake you made, leaving nothing out, and don't try to blame anyone or anything else. To truly own a mistake, you have to accept full responsibility for it. Tell whoever is involved that you understand the mistake was your fault and that you plan to fix it as quickly as you can. If you need help, ask for it and explain why you need it. In many cases, you won't be expected to fix the mistake on your own if others have the ability to help you.

Step 4:

Apologize to anyone affected by your mistake. Apologies go a long way in making things right but be aware that some people may not accept your apology. That's okay. You can only control what's in your power to do, which is to make the apology. You can't force someone to accept it. Just make sure they know you're doing what you can to fix your error so that they have all the information before choosing to accept your apology or not.

Step 5:

Fix the mistake. If you haven't already fixed your mistake, do it now. This shows the people involved that you're serious about making things right. Again, you may need others' help to fix it but

60

don't just leave it in their hands. Ask what you can do to help fix the error and follow through with their suggestions.

Step 6:

Learn from your mistake. As we've already talked about, this is probably the most important part of making a mistake, at least for your own personal growth. You don't want to make the same mistake again.

For example, if you're working with a group at school and you miss a deadline to have your part of the project done, come up with a way to get your work in on time for the next project. Maybe you need to set mini deadlines to have certain parts of your work completed so that it's all done by the final deadline. Perhaps you need to work with a partner who can help remind you to do your part. Your solution might not be what another person would choose, and that's fine as long as it works for you.

RELIABILITY

Think about the people in your life. Who can you trust to do what they say all the time? Who can you rely on to help you if needed? Reliability is a key factor in relationships, and whether you're reliable or not can make or break those relationships. Being reliable means that your actions always align with your words. When you say you're going to do something, you do it even if you don't really want to when the time comes. For example, let's say you agree to go to a movie with a friend on Saturday. The day before that, on

Friday, another friend calls you up and invites you to a party. You might really want to go to the party, but you've already told the other friend you would go to a movie with them. Reliability is saying no to the party and keeping your word to your first friend.

Every time you back out of a commitment, you erode your reputation of being reliable, even if it's just a little bit. Telling your friend you aren't going to go to the movies with them might seem minor, but to that friend, you're no longer as reliable as you once were. They're less likely to trust you again to keep your word the next time they need or want you to do something.

Being reliable doesn't mean saying yes to everything. It just means that you only say yes to what you can follow through on and ensure that you do, in fact, follow through. Having too many commitments actually leads to being less reliable because chances are that you'll miss something or have to bail on a commitment to get everything done. As such, setting boundaries for what you commit to is important for staying reliable.

Of course, there will be times when you can't keep your word, and you'll have to take responsibility for being unreliable. When this happens, own your mistake and try to rebuild trust with the people you let down. For instance, if you did cancel your plans with your first friend to go to the party with the second friend instead, admit to your first friend that you made a mistake and would like to make it up to them. Tell them how you want to make things right and what you intend to do in the future.

62

They might not accept your apology right away, but if you're given the opportunity to be there for that friend again in the future, make sure you keep your promises. It's going to take some time to rebuild trust, but it can happen. Depending on the situation, it will take more time to build trust with some people than with others, but you'll need to be patient and keep working toward that goal.

Being reliable is a fundamental element of responsibility. Be there when you say you'll be there. Do the things you say you're going to do. Don't leave people hanging when they're counting on you to help them. Each time you follow through on your commitments, you're building your reputation for being a responsible and reliable person, something that will open opportunities and create possibilities throughout the rest of your life.

Fun activity suggestion: Make a chore chart and cross off tasks when completed.

CHAPTER SEVEN: TIME MANAGEMENT

A MAN NAMED WOLFGANG

Born in 1756, Wolfgang learned to read and write music by the time he was five years old; by the time he was six, he was writing his own musical compositions. As he grew older, Wolfgang's love of music only strengthened, and in a time when being a musician and composer was unheard of (unless you worked for the king's court or the church), Wolfgang Amadeus Mozart dedicated his life to doing just that.

Mozart loved to compose music, but it didn't pay the bills, so to make ends meet, he gave music lessons. He was also fortunate enough to have numerous wealthy backers who provided for him financially, but that came at a cost: In exchange for their financial support, Mozart had to make regular event appearances.

With so many demands on his time, Mozart kept a strict daily schedule. To earn money, he spent four hours each morning teaching music lessons. To keep his benefactors happy, he spent four hours or more at lunches and parties. And to nurture his love of music, he spent eight hours each day composing. Mozart implemented a daily routine of goal setting and task prioritization to become one of the most successful composers in history, with over 600 works to his name.

Good time management skills are necessary in every aspect of your life, from finishing your homework to nurturing relationships with others. We have limited time each day, and we must use that time wisely. But how do you juggle multiple tasks, nurture relationships, and take time out for yourself? The trick to effective time management is prioritizing tasks, vigilantly monitoring time, and setting goals.

Prioritizing Tasks

Making the most of your time means ensuring you have enough time to do the things you *have* to do and enough time to do the things you *want* to do. It's often easier to do the things we want to do first, but then we're crunched for time when it comes to doing the things we're less excited about doing. This is why learning how to prioritize your tasks is necessary.

Prioritizing involves ranking a list of things like tasks in order of importance, with the first thing on the list designated as most important. The first consideration when prioritizing your tasks is whether they're especially important or urgent. Tasks that are urgent have immediate deadlines that need to be handled right away to avoid further problems. Almost any task can be considered important, or it probably wouldn't even be on your list in the first place. Once you've identified the urgent items on your list, move on to the next criteria, which is often consequences.

Typically, the tasks near the top of the list are those that must be done to avoid unpleasant circumstances. For example, you have three tasks to accomplish after school: vacuum the carpet in your house, finish a worksheet for science that's due tomorrow morning, and watch the newest episode of your favorite television show. The task you probably most want to do is watch the episode of the television show. That's only natural because it's enjoyable. However, what are the consequences if you don't have enough time to finish that task? Probably none, especially since you can likely watch the episode later. That indicates watching the television show should be last on your priority list. On the other hand, what are the consequences if you don't have enough time to vacuum the floor or finish your science worksheet? If you don't vacuum the floor, your parents or guardians might be angry or even ground you. If you don't complete your science worksheet, you'll get a bad grade.

The consequences of not vacuuming and not finishing your worksheet seem fair even, so turn to the next criterion, which is when each task is due. Imagine that your parents told you to vacuum the carpet by 5:00 p.m. or you would be in trouble. Your worksheet won't take very long to complete, and its due date isn't until the next day. As such, it looks like it's more beneficial for you to vacuum the carpet, then complete your worksheet. If you still have time after your worksheet is done, go ahead and watch that television program.

As you can see, the time a task takes to complete can also play a factor in prioritization. Sometimes, it's better to get done with the quick things on your list so that you can focus on the tasks that will take more time. But if you have to make a choice between an urgent task that's going to take a while and an important task that's quick, it's still usually better to take care of the urgent task first.

The best way to prioritize the tasks in your life is to sit down and make a list of everything that has to get done. Use a color-coding system to identify the importance of each item. For example, highlight the urgent items on your list in orange, the important items with more severe consequences in yellow, and the important items with less severe consequences in green.

Learning how to prioritize your tasks is the first step toward improving your time management. You will see a real difference in how much time you have to tackle the urgent items on your list when you put them first. It does mean that sometimes you'll have to leave certain tasks at the bottom of your list undone for a while, but if they're truly important, they'll eventually move up your list.

Manage Your Time Effectively

By prioritizing your tasks, you'll already start managing your time more effectively, but there are some other steps you can take to become even better at this challenging skill. To begin with, humans thrive on routine and organization. We like to have our days planned out so that we know what comes next as we move throughout our day. That's why so many people use a daily planner or calendar of some sort.

You can create a basic schedule for before school, at school, after school, and before bed to help you manage the main part of your day. If you prefer, you can make it more detailed down to every task you need to get done during the day. It really depends on where you currently are with managing your time. If it's something you're okay with but not great, then you may need some structure, but you probably don't have to schedule the time to brush your teeth. If, however, you find yourself daydreaming while you brush your teeth to the point where you miss the bus every day, you probably need a lot of structure. Try scheduling everything for at least a little while until you understand how much time each task should take.

One of the best tools to use is a timer. Some people tend to let time get away with them if they aren't tracking it, and that can lead to spending too much time on one task and not enough time on another. In turn, this leads to rushing to get things done, stress, and missed deadlines. Setting a time to work on one task will help you stay focused and finish it promptly. This is partly why schools use a bell system to signal when it's time to switch classes. Without a bell, teachers might get so involved in what they're teaching, and students so involved in what they're learning, that they forget to change classes. Of course, that's an extreme example, but it does show that setting a timer can help you stick to the schedule you created.

A timer can also help you break up tasks by designating a set amount of time you'll work on a larger task each day or setting intervals to work intermittently until the task is done. The key to successfully breaking up larger tasks is to understand how much time the overall job is going to take.

We often procrastinate or put off doing tasks that are overwhelming, and this causes us to wait until the last minute to tackle something that takes a long time to do. Part of time management is understanding when a task is so large that it needs

70

to be broken down into mini tasks so that you can complete the entire task on time. This is particularly true for chores or jobs that you don't really want to do. Spending a little bit of time working toward the completion of unpleasant tasks is far better than putting them off until you're forced to do it all at once.

Once you start prioritizing your tasks and begin using time management strategies to keep yourself on track, you'll be amazed at how quickly you get things done and how much time you have to devote to things you really want to do. When you don't spend a lot of time procrastinating or complaining about what you need to do, it opens up quite a bit of time to pursue your interests. Plus, you'll notice a reduction in stress and anxiety because you'll have plenty of time to meet all your deadlines.

Fun activity suggestion: Make a schedule for your day and stick to it.

CHAPTER EIGHT: GOAL SETTING

A GIRL NAMED MALALA

In 1997, a little girl named Malala was born in Pakistan. When Malala was three years old, war broke out in neighboring Afghanistan. At the time, an extremist group called the Taliban ruled Afghanistan. The United States waged war and pushed the Taliban out of the country, but the Taliban moved into neighboring Pakistan to plan how to regain control. It took less than a decade for the Taliban to begin taking back Afghan territory.

The Taliban imposed strict lifestyle changes during their time in Pakistan, and one of these changes was to forbid women from getting an education. Throughout her life, Malala's father advocated for education and even ran a chain of public schools. Her father's emphasis on the importance of education significantly impacted Malala, and she began to speak out advocating for education for women.

During her advocacy, Malala wrote an anonymous blog for the BBC about life under the Taliban threat and appeared in a *New York Times* documentary. After the documentary came out, Malala was exposed as the writer of the BBC blog. She was awarded the National Youth Peace Prize in Pakistan and nominated for the International Children's Peace Prize. Malala's high profile and willingness to speak out against the Taliban led to a plot to kill her. One day, a gunman walked onto her school bus and shot her in the head. Malala did not die.

As she lay in the hospital, people worldwide banded together to advocate for women's education, helping to pass the Right to Education in Pakistan. The movement continued to grow, and more people began to advocate for the right to education. After her release from the hospital, Malala delivered a speech in 2013 at the United Nations, supporting those who spoke out in her name and calling for worldwide access to education.

These days, Malala lives in the United Kingdom. She has completed studies at Oxford University and runs her own film and TV production company while traveling the world and speaking out about gender equality. Malala and her father also set up the Malala Fund, dedicated to ensuring that girls get the opportunity to pursue the future they dream of.

Malala had a goal: She wanted girls to get the same educational opportunities as boys. Malala was so dedicated that even after the people she spoke out against shot her, she continued to stand up for change. What began as a local goal eventually snowballed, and now Malala runs her own educational charity and advocates for women's rights globally.

Even if your goals are not as serious as Malala's, setting goals helps you reach important milestones. Achieving goals in school will set you up for success later in life while achieving personal goals ensures you feel happy and fulfilled. The trick to goal setting is to have realistic goals, create a plan to achieve them, and keep striving to reach them.

SETTING REALISTIC GOALS

A goal is something that you strive for, something that you want to accomplish because reaching it will give you a reward. Depending on your goal, that reward might be satisfaction, or it might be something more concrete, like getting your first job. Anything can be a goal, but it's always best to choose something realistic. This might mean that you need to start small and work toward a bigger goal. For example, if you want to be a famous actor or actress, this is a goal that can be difficult to achieve. Instead, it's more realistic to say that you want to go to college to study performing arts. This puts your goal closer to being within reach. You might even start with a smaller milestone, like graduating high school with performing arts experience and a good grade-point average.

Setting more achievable goals may feel like you're thinking small, but by keeping goals to a more realistic level, you're giving yourself the opportunity to succeed. Plus, no one is saying that you can't make new goals after you achieve your first. In the example above, you might make three goals:

- Graduate high school with performing arts experience and a good grade-point average.
- Get into college to study performing arts.
- Become an actor/actress.

Looking at the three milestones above, can you see how it's more achievable and realistic, to begin with something that's a little more within reach? What do you suppose would happen if you simply set one goal — to become a famous actor or actress? This goal is far off into the future, which means striving for something that will take years to realize. It's easy to become discouraged or distracted over the course of years. By setting a goal so far into the future, you're not giving yourself the opportunity to feel gratification at multiple stages.

Gratification is a great motivator, and we feel gratified when we reach our goals. If you manage to graduate high school with performing arts experience and a good grade-point average, you get to feel that incredible sense of accomplishment. You get to feel like you've made progress, which fuels you to keep pushing forward to meet your next goal: getting into college to study performing arts.

However, even setting smaller, more attainable goals can feel overwhelming at times, which is why it's always a good idea to come up with a plan to achieve your goals.

Question: What goals do you have for the future?

77

Develop a Plan to Achieve Your Goals

Developing a plan to achieve your goals helps break down your goal into bite-sized pieces.

A famous man named Desmond Tutu once said that the only way to eat an elephant is one bite at a time. Of course, he wasn't actually talking about eating an elephant, but he was talking about tackling a big project. Sometimes, that big project can feel overwhelming, but when we break it down one bite at a time, it becomes something we can manage.

How can you begin breaking your elephant into bite-sized pieces? Let's look at the example we used before: becoming an actor or actress.

Your first goal is to graduate high school with performing arts experience and a good grade-point average. It's a good idea to sit down with a pen and paper or your tablet to begin planning how you can achieve that goal. For example, you might begin like this:

- Find out my current grade point average.
- If my grade point average isn't satisfactory, find out how I can bring it up so that I can graduate with a high grade-point average.
- Find out what productions the school drama program is doing in the coming months/years and how I can audition for a part.
- Find out if there are any drama classes that I can take in school for additional performing arts experience.

- Find out if there's a drama club that I can take part in after school for added experience.

Listing out your plan of attack this way is helpful because it lets you go back and reference your plan in the future. It's also a good idea to make notes under each step to organize your thoughts and give yourself more direction. For example, under the first step, you might want to make the following notes:

- Can I find out my GPA by logging onto the school website?
- If not, who do I need to contact to find out my current GPA?
- If I need to bring my current GPA up, who can I talk to that might be able to help me do that?

Once you start working on your directions for all your goals, you might realize that there's something you forgot to include in your list. In our example, you may realize that in order to go to college, you need to save up money. You may go back and add another goal to your list to get a part-time job and save up money for college. It's not uncommon to have to go back and reassess goals or make adjustments to your current plan to account for things you may have forgotten. You may also need to go back and make changes to your goals if things don't turn out the way you hope.

Question: Can you think of a different way to break down your goals into smaller, bite-sized pieces?

Persevere and Keep Trying

Things don't always turn out the way we want. When that happens, you have two choices: You can give up and abandon your goals, or you can go back, reassess, and try again. In our example of becoming an actor or actress, for example, you may not get accepted into a performing arts program because they had too many applicants that year. So, what do you do next? There's a good chance that you still want to become an actor or actress—not getting into a program shouldn't change that if you're serious about your goal. Now, looking at the two choices you have, does it make sense to give up and abandon your dream of becoming an actor or actress? Or does it make more sense to go back and reassess your plan of action and see if there's another way to pursue your goal?

If you decide that you still very much want to be an actor or actress, look back at your goal and your plan to achieve it. You have already decided that you still want to pursue the same goal, so that stays the same, but is there anything you can change about your plan to achieve it? You may find that you don't need to change anything about your plan of action either. For example, if you didn't get into the NYU performing arts program because there were too many applicants, but you were still a good candidate, maybe all you need to do is try again during the next application period.

On the other hand, if you did not get into a performing arts program because your qualifications didn't meet the requirements of top schools, you might choose to rework your plan a little. For example, you might:

- Decide to apply to other performing arts programs that aren't quite as competitive
- Take a year or two to get more experience in performing arts to improve your chances of getting into a top program the next time you apply
- Take time to work in the performing arts to get work experience
- Take more classes in performing arts to improve your chances

Sometimes, having to rework our plans can be disappointing. For example, if you discover that your chances of being accepted to a top-performing arts program are very low, you may be disappointed that you have to apply to other schools. If you feel yourself getting disappointed over having to make changes to your plan, it's a good idea to take a moment to remind yourself why this change isn't the end of the world. Writing a list can help. In our example above, you may write the following list:

- I'm still a good candidate for three other top-performing arts programs that aren't as competitive.
- There are famous actors and actresses who attended these other performing arts programs and still made a name for themselves in Hollywood.
- It might be cheaper to attend a less competitive performing arts program, and that means less debt in the future.

This list serves as encouragement to keep you on track and remind you to keep pushing forward even if things didn't go the way you imagined. You can still wind up where you want to be in the end.

Fun activity suggestion: Write a letter to your future self with your goals and how you plan to achieve them.

CHAPTER NINE: FINANCIAL LITERACY

A MAN NAMED ANDREW

Andrew was born in Scotland in 1835. When he was 13 years old, his family sold their belongings and moved into a couple of rooms above a weaving shop owned by relatives in Pennsylvania. Andrew's father eventually took over the business, but it failed, leaving the family in need again. To help support his family, Andrew got work at a local cotton mill, earning $1.20 weekly.

The following year, Andrew got hired by a telegraph company, where he took the opportunity to learn about telegraph technology. By furthering his education, Andrew earned himself a promotion to an operator position and eventually got a job at the Pennsylvania Railroad. At age 24, Andrew was the superintendent.

Even while working long hours, Andrew read every book he could find and continued to educate himself, intent on bettering his life. Taking advantage of self-teaching and opportunities presented to him through his work at the railroad, Andrew began to invest in projects and businesses and buy stock. Over the years, Andrew's fortune began to swell, and by 1901, it grew exponentially when he sold his steel company.

Andrew Carnegie went from a life of poverty to being one of the wealthiest men in the world through hard work and teaching himself financial literacy.

84

Financial literacy is necessary for any successful adult. You need to know how to earn money, how to use the money you earn, and how to ensure your money lasts. However, don't confuse financial literacy with financial success. Everyone wants financial success, but financial success doesn't come without first becoming financially literate. So how do you become financially literate when you don't know where to begin? The trick is learning to budget and save while working hard.

BUDGET YOUR MONEY

Financial literacy is a critical skill that everyone needs to know, but very few schools teach it, so here's your quick overview. It starts with budgeting. You've probably heard the term before, but you may not understand exactly what it means.

Whether you have a job or a regular allowance, you have money coming in on a predictable schedule. You need to be able to use that money responsibly. Budgeting is how you decide to spend or save it.

For example, if you get an allowance of $20 a week, that means you get $80 every month. Now, if you also have a cell phone that costs $50 a month, you have to use your money wisely to make sure you can pay that cell phone bill every month. This is called budgeting.

You might save your allowance for the first three weeks of the month so that you have $60 saved up and can pay the $50 for your cell phone bill when it's due. You can then take the $30 you have left over and use it as you see fit.

Why is budgeting important? Budgeting ensures that you pay for obligations like bills when they're due. Paying your bills when they're due is not only part of being responsible, but it also helps you build your financial record for the future.

If you budget your money well and pay your cell phone bill on time every month for the four years that you're in high school, you will have built a reliable record of financial responsibility. Once it's time to graduate high school, you may decide that you want to buy a car so that you can get around town while you attend college or start a job. Since you probably don't have the money saved to buy a car outright, you'll need to look into borrowing the money you need.

When you go to the car dealership and ask them to loan you the money to buy a car, they're going to look at your financial history. If the dealership looks at your history and sees that you've paid your bills on time for the past four years, they'll see that you're reliable and less of a risk if they loan you the money you need. If, however, you missed payments and developed a poor financial record, do you think the car dealership would be willing to loan you the money on the same terms?

If the car dealership loans you the money you need, you can then buy your car and pay back the loan in monthly installments. That way, you don't have to come up with a lot of money all at once.

SAVE YOUR MONEY

Budgeting is important to your financial record, which is also called your credit rating, but you don't want to spend your whole life borrowing money and having to pay it back. When you borrow money, you have to pay that money back each month with interest. Interest is like a fee that you pay for borrowing money, and it's usually a percentage of the money you borrowed. For example, if you have five years to pay back $15,000 with 14.5 percent interest, that means you'll have 60 monthly payments on your loan. If you just have to pay back what you borrowed, those monthly payments would be $250, but since you're also paying interest of 14.5 percent, you'll end up paying an extra $6,175.45 over those 60 months—or an extra $102.92 every month. That's a lot of extra money to pay just for the privilege of borrowing money!

But how can you cut down the amount of money you pay each year? By saving! If you save your money, you can reduce the amount of money that you need to borrow to buy your car, which also reduces your interest.

People save money in different ways, but one of the best is to set up a savings account with a local bank. Your parents or guardians can help you do this. Once you set up your savings account, you can then make regular deposits into that account every month. In the example above, you might decide to take the $30 you have left over every month and put it into your savings account. After four years of putting $30 into your savings account every month, you should have $1,440 in your account.

But wait, there's good news! Interest isn't just something that you pay; it's also something that you can earn. This is why savings accounts are a great idea because they pay you interest on the money that you have in your account. The bank pays interest because it's using your money while it's in savings. Your money is still there when you want to take it out, but the bank can use it in the meantime to make their own investments and make money for themselves.

If you deposit $30 every month and the bank pays you interest, by the time you go to take all of that money out of your account, you will have more than $1,440 — perhaps around $1,500.

You can use that $1,500 as a down payment on your car. A down payment is an amount of money that you pay upfront toward your car so that you borrow less money. So, in our example, you would only have to borrow about $13,500 from the car dealership to buy your car. That means you would only wind up paying $5,557 in interest. It's still a hefty chunk of money but saving money for a down payment means that you pay less to borrow it.

The more money you're able to save, the less money you wind up paying for the privilege of borrowing when you do need to borrow money.

Work Hard to Earn Money

Budgeting your money is one way to save more, but another great way is to earn more in the first place. Working hard to earn more money lets you save more, which means that you earn more interest from the bank and pay less interest when you borrow money for a purchase. In an ideal world, you can work hard and earn enough money to pay for your purchase without borrowing money at all.

Fun activity suggestion: Play a game where you budget for a pretend vacation.

CHAPTER TEN: THE IMPORTANCE OF EDUCATION

A MAN NAMED FREDERICK

Frederick was born into slavery in 1818 and sent to live with his grandmother, as his mother was a valuable plantation asset. In 1826, Frederick was uprooted and sent to work on a plantation in Talbot County, Maryland. After a year of driving cattle at the plantation owner's farms, Frederick was given to a family in Baltimore to keep their young child company. The Auld family didn't own any slaves before Frederick, and Mrs. Auld was kind to Frederick and even began teaching him to read. When Mr. Auld discovered that his wife was teaching Frederick to read, he became angry, and she was no longer permitted to teach Frederick.

Although Frederick no longer had his reading teacher, he'd already developed a desire to learn, and he understood that to be a free man, he must become educated. So, Frederick started to carry around a spelling book and give whatever he could afford to neighborhood children in exchange for reading lessons. Once Frederick could read, he taught other slaves to read too. By the time he was 12, Frederick had saved enough money to buy *The Columbian Orator* journal, and, reading its articles, he began to build his knowledge of human rights and learned about abolition. Later in life, Frederick is quoted as saying, "Once you learn to read, you will be forever free."

When he was around 16, Frederick went to live with another local slave owner named William Freeland. When more people realized that Frederick was teaching other slaves to read, he got transferred

92

again, this time to a violent slave owner named Edward Covey. Frederick tried to escape Covey's possession many times, but when he was 20 years old, he finally succeeded. Frederick boarded a train in Maryland, traveled to a safe house in New York, and eventually married and settled in Massachusetts, where he played a lead role in the abolitionist movement. In 1860, Frederick published his first autobiography, *Narrative of the Life of Frederick Douglass, an American Slave.*

Education was the key to Frederick Douglass's escape from a life of slavery, but it also empowered him to educate others and make a big difference in the world. Even once freed, Frederick continued to educate others, writing two autobiographies, advancing the abolitionist movement, and standing up for women's right to vote.

DEVELOPING A LOVE FOR LEARNING

By paying attention in school and developing a love for learning, you have the knowledge and means to achieve any goal you set for yourself and the opportunity to educate others. Education is a lifelong endeavor; you should never stop learning.

Often, people who love learning and have a strong desire to continue their education throughout their lives have people in their inner circle who model this value. Teachers and parents are two of the strongest advocates for education that you'll have in your life, but if you don't have someone to help you develop a love for learning, you can still do it on your own. In fact, wanting to learn new things and becoming a lifelong learner are values you can add to your life at any age.

If you aren't already someone who loves to learn new things, it might be because you're trying to learn them in a way that doesn't work for you. Everyone learns things differently, including you. Some people are visual learners who need to see concepts in a visual presentation before they understand them. Others are aural learners who can absorb new material just by listening to someone explain it to them. Still, others are hands-on learners who need to physically engage with the material before they can fully grasp new concepts. There are even verbal learners who learn best by repeating material out loud so that their brains have to process the information twice: once when they speak it and once when they hear it.

Take an online quiz to see what type of learner you are, and use that information to tackle new concepts and material. You'll probably discover that the job of learning is much more pleasant when you do it in a way that makes sense to you.

Another way to help you develop a love of learning is to choose topics that you're interested in and want to know more about. You'll naturally push yourself to learn as much as possible about topics you like, and you can usually find ways to incorporate skills you need to know into just about any subject you're interested in learning about.

For example, if you enjoy learning about dinosaurs and the world they lived in but you're not as inspired by math, it's possible to learn math skills by creating math equations that relate to dinosaurs. Perhaps you can calculate how long ago they lived or determine the scale of dinosaurs to current animals. These math skills are ones you'll use frequently throughout your life, but you can learn the processes required to solve these equations by studying something you already love.

As you move through school, you'll start to narrow your classes from those that impart general knowledge to those that teach more specific knowledge, so keep that in mind as you think about the things you want to study. As soon as you get the opportunity to choose elective classes, do so with intention so that you pick the ones you're most interested in, thereby keeping you engaged with learning new things.

It's also beneficial to take opportunities to learn outside of school. Go to those camps over the summer. Participate in after-school clubs. Attend free workshops at the library or community center. These types of opportunities give you a chance to discover your interests. Then you can seek out other educational programs that focus more on what you want to learn in addition to what you have to learn during your school day.

EDUCATION AND SUCCESS

Most life goals require some form of education. This means that for each step you take toward a goal, there may be an element of education involved. Some steps require less education than others,

95

but to attain the final goal, you will have accumulated a lot of knowledge between when you started and when you finished.

For instance, if you have a goal of becoming a veterinarian, there are specific educational requirements you must fulfill before you can actually treat animals. Those steps all have education tied to them.

Step 1: Finish high school with a grade-point average that allows you to enroll in a college or university.

Step 2: Take classes related to veterinary science. These might include biology, chemistry, animal science, zoology, and others. In each class, you'll obtain new skills that move you toward your ultimate goal.

Step 3: Attain your undergraduate degree, which includes the prerequisite knowledge required to enroll in a veterinary school. There are only a few schools that offer a Doctor of Veterinary Medicine degree.

Step 4: Complete a Doctor of Veterinary Medicine degree.

Step 5: Pass any applicable licensing exams. You should have all the knowledge necessary to pass these exams from the previous steps building up to this one, but you can't just jump to this step without completing the previous steps.

Step 5: Take additional classes to specialize in an aspect of veterinarian such as large animals, farm animals, or research. This might also be where you take a residency class that allows you to learn more about the profession while shadowing an experienced veterinarian.

No matter what career you choose, you'll need at least some education, whether it's formal education like you get in school or informal education that you get when you train for a specific job. Most of the time, it's a combination of both, with some careers requiring more formal education and others requiring more training. When you decide the career path you want, you'll be able to set your goals and create the steps you'll need to complete to get there.

Education also helps you set your goals because you'll learn about jobs and careers that you wouldn't otherwise know about as you study general subjects in school. You might not know exactly what you want to do right now, and that's okay. There will come a time when you learn about a career you never knew about, and it will become your goal. The more knowledge you have, the easier it is to avoid jobs and careers you know you don't want.

When you graduate from high school, go to college, graduate from college, and pursue your career, you're also gaining "soft" skills like persistence and perseverance that are necessary to reach all types of goals. Failure can lead you down two paths. One path is quitting before you reach your goal, and the other path is learning from failure. Education helps you choose the second path more often than not.

School Is Important for Your Future

Sometimes, you might wonder why you go to school at all, especially if you haven't had a good experience. You might think school is just a place for you to go while your parents or guardians are at work. But the truth is that school is important for your future. Once you learn something, no one can take that knowledge from you. You will always have your education, no matter what life throws at you. The more education you have, the more options you'll have for what you can do with your life. It opens up opportunities you might not expect and takes you in completely different directions to help you find meaning in what you do. Quite simply, education opens doors that are often closed to people with less education.

Not only does education give you more opportunities in life, but it also teaches you skills that you'll use for the rest of your life. Yes, you're learning content, but you're also learning skills like teamwork, communication, problem-solving, critical thinking, professionalism, creativity, and more. These are skills that all employers look for, so learning them at a young age and practicing them throughout school is vital for your future success.

Typically, more education also translates to a higher income. Of course, this depends on the career field you ultimately go into, but the higher-paying jobs in society generally require more education or training. This doesn't mean you have to go to college to get a high-paying job. It just means you need to have the right education to perform those high-paying jobs, whether that's going to college, entering an apprenticeship program, or attending a trade school.

Education also levels the playing field. Think back to Frederick Douglass. Without education, he was destined to be a slave for the rest of his life, as were all the other slaves Douglass eventually taught to read. By teaching himself as much as he could about history and the way the world worked, Douglass was able to show others that he was their equal, something that was extremely hard for a Black person to do in the 1800s.

Overall, education gives you the tools to create the life you want. It gives you choices that people without an education just don't have. Always try to take advantage of the educational opportunities you find because it can never hurt to have more knowledge. The more you know, the more you can do and the more satisfied you'll be with your life.

Fun activity suggestion: Visit a museum or science center to learn new things.

CHAPTER ELEVEN: SELF-ADVOCACY

A WOMAN NAMED ROSA

Rosa was born on February 4, 1913, in Tuskegee, Alabama. As a child, she attended an industrial school for girls. Rosa lived with her grandparents, who were both former slaves and strong supporters of the racial equality movement. As a Black child during a time of great segregation, Rosa experienced a lot of discrimination; she often spoke of her early memories of watching hate groups march down her street while her grandfather stood at the door of their home with a shotgun to keep his family safe.

From an early age, Rosa began to follow her grandparents' example and became a strong supporter of racial equality and the civil rights movement. When she married her husband, Raymond, an active figure in the fight for equal rights, Rosa became even more dedicated to social justice. In 1955, Rosa became one of the most historic figures in the civil rights movement when she refused to give up her seat on a Montgomery bus.

After finishing work as a seamstress at the Montgomery Fair department store in Montgomery, Alabama, Rosa Parks boarded a bus on December 1, 1955. At the time, Black passengers were forced to sit at the very back of the bus, and the front ten rows of seats were reserved for white people. Rosa sat in the 11th row. As the bus filled up and there was no more room in the first ten rows, the bus driver asked everyone seated in row 11 to move further back. Everyone except Rosa changed seats, but Rosa simply said no and refused to move. Frustrated at her refusal, the bus driver told Rosa that he would call the police and have her arrested. Rosa replied, "You may do that." When the police arrived, Rosa was arrested and fined.

Although she was arrested and forced to pay a $10 fine, Rosa Parks's refusal to move on that day became one of the most significant events contributing to the civil rights movement. Her protest inspired other civil rights leaders to act, and Reverend Dr. Martin Luther King Jr. led a year-long boycott of Montgomery buses by the Black community. When the U.S. Supreme Court stepped in and ruled that segregation on buses was unconstitutional, the boycott ended.

Self-advocacy is an important life skill. It ensures that you are heard and valued, and it teaches you how to advocate for those who cannot advocate for themselves. If Rosa hadn't spoken up and advocated for her rights on that Montgomery bus, she wouldn't have started the ball rolling for other civil rights leaders like Reverend Doctor Martin Luther King Jr. Standing up for yourself isn't always easy, but you're the only one who can speak up for your rights, just like Rosa Parks! Sometimes, you have to self-advocate, and the trick to self-advocacy is respecting yourself and others, being assertive when necessary, and speaking up for yourself.

SPEAK UP FOR YOURSELF

Have you ever had a really good idea, but someone else told you all the reasons why your idea wouldn't work? It can be very discouraging, and that can make you abandon your idea altogether. Imagine if Rosa Parks had told the people on that bus in Montgomery about her idea not to move seats. You can bet there were plenty of them who would have discouraged her. Many passengers would have told her what a bad idea it was to stand up for herself and that she should keep quiet and not cause a scene.

But if Rosa Parks hadn't pushed for civil rights that day on the Montgomery bus, Reverend Doctor Martin Luther King Jr. might not have spoken out for civil rights so boldly and facilitated the boycott. And if King wasn't as active in the civil rights movement, the legislation that led to the Civil Rights Act and Voting Rights Act may not have come about.

- Without the Civil Rights Act of 1964, people could still be treated unfairly based on their race, religion, nationality, or gender.
- Without the Voting Rights Act of 1965, many people would be unable to vote simply because of their race.

So how can you learn to speak up for yourself like Rosa Parks? The first step is knowing when to push back.

104

KNOW WHEN TO PUSH BACK

Have you ever had a really good idea, but when you tell someone else, they explain why it isn't a good idea? That happens to all of us and gives us a chance to improve. You can use that constructive feedback to make your idea even better. For example, imagine that you invented a new type of dog food, and you share your idea with a friend. They tell you that it sounds like a good idea, but you need to do some more research on your recipes because all your dog food recipes contain onions—something that's toxic to dogs. So now you have to decide whether you should push back and defend your recipes or whether your friend has given you advice worth listening to.

In this situation, let's assume you listen to your friend, and you decide to look up how you can change your recipes to make them dog friendly. Learning to accept and use feedback from other people, like in the example above, is an important part of being an adult and becoming a better person. Taking constructive feedback and learning from it has the following benefits:

- You become a better listener and learn to listen when someone else is contributing to your idea.
- You learn new information. Listening to other people's suggestions can teach you something new.

- You become more approachable. People will want to share their ideas with you more often because you value their feedback.

In our example, your friend's advice helped you make a better dog food recipe and stopped you from potentially making your dog sick.

But what about situations when people tell you that your idea is bad when you aren't so sure that it is? At moments like this, take a moment and ask yourself a few questions.

1. *Is this person misunderstanding me or unfamiliar with the situation?*

   For example, imagine someone told you that your dog food idea was a bad one because people can't make their own dog food.

   In this situation, you might politely correct them by explaining that many people make their own dog food at home.

2. *Is this person trying to help even though they see things differently?*

   Imagine your friend told you that your dog food idea was a bad one because the only good food for dogs is raw meat.

   In this situation, listen to what they have to say. If you still feel like your idea is good, but you'll never be able to convince them, thank them for their feedback, and realize that you can't agree all the time.

3. *Is this person disagreeing with me just to disagree with me?*

Imagine your friend told you that your dog food idea was a bad one, but you feel like your friend is disagreeing with you just to disagree.

You need to decide whether it's the right time to stand up for yourself and defend your idea. What is the cost if you push back and assert yourself? Is it worth that cost to push back?

BE ASSERTIVE

Standing up for yourself and asking for what you need is only part of the self-advocacy equation. This is because *how* you ask for what you need is as important as doing it in the first place. People have different ideas of what assertiveness means and looks like. Assertiveness is often confused with aggression, but one is respectful, and one is not. You will rarely get what you want by being aggressive, and even if you do, it might only be because the other person fears you or just wants to appease you so that you'll leave them alone. In either case, the other person probably won't want to help you out again in the future if they ever have the opportunity to do so.

Being aggressive pushes people away, and instead of seeing your request as self-advocacy, people might think you're just being selfish or difficult. For example, if you demand that your teacher give you extra time for an assignment instead of asking politely and explaining why you need it, they may assume that you procrastinated and say no. When you're aggressive instead of assertive, it comes across as putting your own needs above everyone else, especially the person you're being aggressive toward. This might not be the truth at all, but unfortunately, aggressive behavior turns people away from wanting to help you reach your goals.

The opposite of assertiveness is timidity, and as with aggressiveness, it's important to avoid the extreme when standing up for yourself. Being timid isn't going to get you what you need because people might not take you seriously or believe that your needs are as important. Timidity is almost always overshadowed by aggressiveness, so if someone is aggressively demanding what they need and you're timidly asking for it, the aggressive person is often going to get their needs met instead, especially if they're in conflict with each other.

An example of being too timid when advocating for yourself would be if your teacher asked the entire class to say where they need to sit in the classroom to best see the board at the front of the room. Instead of speaking up for yourself and saying, "I have trouble seeing from the back, so I need to sit in the front or second row," you say nothing at all or something like, "I can always walk up to the board if I need to see it better, so just put my desk wherever you want."

People who are timid usually end up regretting the choice that another person made for them. Sure, you could get up from your desk every time you can't see the board, but why should you have to? Your needs are just as important as everyone else's, and your teacher wants to know what you need to be successful in their class.

You know yourself better than anyone else, and your teacher isn't going to know that you have trouble seeing the board from the back unless you say so. Be confident and let them know that having your desk upfront will help you be successful. You don't need to demand that it be moved to the front row but giving them the choice of the front or second row allows them to be flexible in their seating arrangement so that other kids' needs are also met. In this way, you're standing up for your needs, but you're also being respectful of others' needs as well.

RESPECT YOURSELF AND OTHERS

Learning how to stand up for yourself and be assertive means understanding that you deserve to get what you need to be successful. You're learning to respect yourself and have the mindset that your opinions, values, and feelings are just as valid as everyone else's. When you have a healthy sense of self-respect, you're able to take care of yourself emotionally and physically.

Part of advocating for yourself is setting boundaries so that you don't allow yourself to be used or abused by other people. You

109

assertively let people know what behaviors you will and won't accept from them. This allows you to continue on your personal life journey in the healthiest way possible. For instance, in a group project at school, there will probably be some tasks you would rather do than others. Someone who respects themselves will set boundaries with other members of the group by letting them know which tasks they're more comfortable doing and why. They also allow others to do the same. This doesn't mean there won't be conflict over who does which tasks, but it does mean that everyone's needs are being considered and respected, including your own.

While it's vital that you respect yourself and your own needs, it's just as necessary for you to respect others and their needs. This is where assertiveness versus aggressiveness comes into play. An aggressive self-advocate cares only about their needs and getting their way no matter what. An assertive self-advocate expresses their needs, explains why they have those needs and offers solutions that take others' needs into account.

Think about the group project example. Pretend you're most successful in projects when you're assigned the task of interviewing experts to support the group's research. This is because you aren't a great writer, but you can record the interviewees' answers and use those recordings to create a multimedia presentation. However, because writing isn't your best skill, you know you (and ultimately the group) won't be as successful if you're assigned the task of writing the script for the video.

110

Asking for the task of the interviewer for the project is respecting yourself. But to be a true advocate, you also have to respect others. Allow them to express what they need to be successful in the project. If the stars align, you'll all be able to do the task you want, and the project will go off without a hitch. But in most cases, that's not going to happen. There will usually need to be some negotiation involved if multiple group members need the same things. For instance, there may be someone in your group who is physically unable to write and requires the task of the interviewer to be successful. While that's your need as well, you can physically write, so you'll need to identify another task that will allow you to be successful in a different way.

Respecting the needs of others while advocating for your own needs takes practice. At first, many people want what they need without worrying about others. In that group project, for example, if you say you need the role of the interviewer and tell others what roles they're going to do without listening to their needs, you're being aggressive and not very respectful. Expecting everyone to respect your needs without returning that respect is a recipe for a poor group project experience.

Fun activity suggestion: Practice standing up for yourself in different scenarios.

CHAPTER TWELVE: PUTTING IT ALL TOGETHER

A PERSON NAMED YOU

Now that you've reached the final chapter of this book, it's time to stop talking about others and start talking about yourself.

The famous people described in this book are famous because they used at least some of the same advice you've been given here to create the lives they wanted for themselves. They kept a positive outlook no matter the challenges they encountered and developed a growth mindset that allowed them to learn from their mistakes and overcome their obstacles.

These men and women were curious and weren't afraid to try new things, even if they didn't succeed at first. When they encountered difficulties in their lives, they didn't give up. In fact, they tried even harder, knowing that nothing worth doing ever comes easy. They learned to manage their time well, owned their mistakes, and set achievable goals to measure their progress.

Many of these outstanding people weren't born into wealthy families, but they understood the value of a dollar from an early age and worked hard to earn their fortunes. No one was given anything, but these individuals learned how to ask for what they needed.

In the life of every person discussed here, education was a priority. Not all of them excelled at school, but they did excel at finding their passion and pursuing it by gaining knowledge about that passion. Most of them had formal education, but even those who didn't were driven by their need to know more. They read a lot, researched even more, and never stopped learning.

You aren't any different from these remarkable people. You have the tools to become successful in whatever you do. That being said, the advice given here isn't a magic key to success—you will have to work at it—but if you practice the skills in each chapter, you'll get closer to creating the life you want.

This doesn't mean you're going to be famous if you follow all the advice here. That isn't the point of this book. But who knows? You have the capability to do anything you want, so if being famous is your goal, then by all means, shoot for the stars!

In the end, the advice in this book is meant to give you options in life because the best life is one that you make for yourself. It's one where you have a career that fulfills you, a robust circle of friends who respect you and each other, and a healthy sense of self-worth from knowing that you deserve to be successful.

WHO ARE YOU?

What defines who you are as a person? If you could describe yourself by listing ten qualities or characteristics, what would they be?

Come up with a list of 10 positive things that make up who you are. Here are some examples to get you started:

- I'm good at making people laugh.
- I'm not afraid to speak in front of a crowd.
- I like solving math problems.
- I know a lot about Minecraft.
- I'm a very fast reader.
- I'm part of a culturally diverse family.
- I'm always kind.
- I always try to make good decisions.
- I'm very good with animals.
- I always encourage my friends.

Focusing on your positive attributes is a great way to remind yourself of your worth.

Now come up with a list of 10 things you might want to work on, such as:

- I'm a bit messy.
- I can be very loud sometimes.
- I sometimes get angry too quickly.
- I don't go outside a lot.
- I'm easily discouraged.
- I can be impatient.
- I'm always late.
- I sometimes interrupt others.
- I don't always listen in class.
- I don't like losing.

Focusing on your negative attributes is a great way to encourage yourself to make changes and grow as a person.

Do you love and accept yourself for who you are?

Do you love yourself and accept yourself for those positive qualities? Do you remind yourself of your worth every day? If you do not, try to practice coming up with a positive quality about yourself every morning before you get out of bed.

How do you manage your negative thoughts and feelings?

Do you think too much about those negative qualities and start to feel discouraged or sad? If you find yourself stuck thinking about your negative qualities, take a moment to "turn down the volume" on the noise. Remind yourself that everyone has negative qualities, but it's what you do once you recognize them that matters. Are you happy to let your negative qualities define you, or is there something you could do to change them so that you can scratch them off your list?

Look at your list of 10 negative qualities and try to come up with a way that you could change them to take them off your list. For example, with our list above, you might say:

- I'm a bit messy, but I can change this by remembering to clean up after myself anytime I make a mess.
- I can be very loud sometimes, but I can change this by stopping to think before I talk.

- I sometimes get angry too quickly, but I can change this by counting to 10 and trying to understand why I feel angry and whether it's something worth being angry about.
- I don't go outside a lot, but I can change this by going out with my family on weekends instead of staying at home to play video games.
- I'm easily discouraged, but I can change this by reminding myself that criticism and loss are opportunities to improve and grow.
- I can be impatient, but I can change this by reminding myself to be patient because sometimes people have other things on their minds or other things to do.
- I'm always late, but I can change this by setting my alarm 10 minutes earlier so that I have time to finish what I need to do and still be on time.
- I sometimes interrupt others, but I can change this by waiting for someone else to stop speaking before I start.
- I don't always listen in class, but I can change this by reminding myself how important my education is to my success in the future.
- I don't like losing, but I can change this by reminding myself that I can't win all the time, and losing gives me a chance to improve.

In each of the examples above, we took a negative characteristic and turned it into a positive. Sometimes, it can be difficult to change things about ourselves, but as long as you keep working on bettering yourself, you can always say that you're trying your best!

Do you take care of yourself?

Even when you try your best, you might sometimes fall short, and that might make you feel discouraged. Everyone feels discouraged at times; keeping a positive mindset isn't always easy! But part of being positive is realizing that you're human and you might fail. Accept this fact and give yourself grace. Remind yourself that you tried, and you can always try again. You have many positive qualities; make determination one of them.

Are you self-confident?

Being determined is a key factor in building self-confidence. It can be difficult to find the motivation to keep going when things don't go your way, but if you have confidence in yourself and push yourself to learn from your mistakes, you will quickly become more self-assured.

Do you try new things and take risks?

Trying new things and taking risks is something that self-confident people often do because it gives them a chance to have more experiences and grow as a person. Sometimes, if we lack self-confidence, though, we can be hesitant to step outside of our comfort zones.

Do you try new things and take risks, or do you prefer not to step out of your comfort zone? Staying in your comfort zone may feel better, but what might you miss out on if you don't have the confidence to try something new and take risks?

119

Come up with a list of five new things you can try that will help you to grow as a person. For example, you might include:

- Being the first person to apologize when you have a disagreement, even if you don't think you were in the wrong
- Trying to put yourself in someone else's shoes when you listen to them talk
- Doing something nice for someone without expecting anything in return
- Listening to and recognizing merits in someone's argument even when you don't agree with their point of view
- Speaking up when you see someone being treated unfairly, even if you're uncomfortable being assertive

Are you inclusive and accepting of others?

Many of the examples above require you to be inclusive and accepting of others. Sometimes, it can be difficult to let go of our own perspective and see things from someone else's, but if you listen, you might just learn a thing or two and broaden your own horizons.

Do you listen to others?

Listening to others is one of the best ways to show acceptance. It's also a great way to ensure clear communication and build new friendships. How could you be a better listener?

120

Do you express yourself effectively?

Being a good listener is just one-half of good communication; you also have to express yourself effectively.

- Do you speak clearly?
- Do you always say what you mean?
- Do you overcomplicate things when speaking?
- Do you over-explain?
- Do you speak quickly or without pausing?

What could you do to better communicate with others?

Are you kind, and do you empathize with others?

Good communication isn't only about speaking clearly and listening; it's also about *how* you listen. Are you kind and empathetic? Do you take time to listen to someone and offer genuine feedback? Do you imagine how you would feel if you were in their position?

Have you built and maintained friendships?

Being kind and empathetic are both traits that make building friendships easier. Don't you find it easier to talk to and be around someone who's aware of how you feel and considerate of those feelings?

Do you think others would say you're a good friend? What do you think you could do to be a better friend?

Do you talk and work through problems?

Friendships can be complicated, and we sometimes have disagreements or run into problems with others. It's important to talk about and work through these problems to maintain friendships.

When you have problems with your friends, do you talk to them about it? Do you try to work through problems together or just ignore them until they go away?

If you normally ignore problems, try working through them by talking next time. Explain your feelings and why you did what you did, then take time to listen to the other person and put yourself in their shoes.

Do you learn from your mistakes?

Sometimes, problems in friendships occur because we make mistakes. It can be difficult, but it's important to any relationship that you're able to admit to your mistakes and learn from them. Admitting mistakes lets your friend know that you recognize you were wrong; learning from your mistakes means you learned from the experience and don't want to repeat it again.

What was the last mistake you remember making, and what did you learn from it?

Do you take responsibility for your actions?

Taking responsibility for our mistakes is important, but so is taking responsibility for our actions. Part of being an adult is being able to admit to your actions and take ownership of the consequences.

Do you handle setbacks and failures well?

Another important part of being an adult is being able to handle setbacks and failures well. For example, you should be able to admit that something failed but continue working on it to get a successful outcome.

When something fails, do you get frustrated or angry? Do you keep working to get the answer you're looking for? If you don't handle setbacks and failure well, what could you do to handle them better?

Are you resilient and determined?

Being willing to pursue something despite setbacks and failure shows resilience and determination—both important character traits in adult life. Do you bounce back quickly when things don't go your way and keep trying when you fail? Or do you throw up your hands and quit?

What's an example of a time when you could have been more resilient or determined? What could you have done better?

Are you reliable?

Reliability is just as important as resilience and determination. People rely on you every single day. Maybe you have teammates who rely on you to participate during games, or maybe your family depends on you to finish certain chores.

Could you be more reliable? What do you think you could do to prove your reliability?

Do you set goals and work toward them?

Setting goals and working toward them is one way that you can prove your reliability. Goals provide you with motivation and show your willingness to invest yourself into achieving a certain outcome.

Do you have any current goals? If so, what is your top goal, and how are you working toward it?

Are your goals realistic, and do you have a plan to achieve them?

Setting goals is important, but it's just as important to set goals that are realistic. How would you feel if every goal you set was so far out of reach that you never achieved any of them? You'd probably feel very discouraged, setting yourself up for failure! By setting realistic goals and coming up with a plan to achieve them, however, you can set yourself up for success. Success provides motivation to keep driving forward.

124

Do you manage your time effectively and prioritize tasks?

Achieving goals requires dedication, but it also requires good time management skills and task prioritization. For example, if you have three tasks to do to meet your goal and 30 minutes to finish them, then it makes sense to dedicate 10 minutes to each task. You might also do the easier tasks first so that any "leftover time" from those tasks can be used for the more challenging job.

Do you usually manage your time well, or do you always find yourself running out of time? If you always run out of time, what could you do to better manage it?

Do you persevere when things don't go as planned?

Even when you manage your time well and prioritize tasks, things don't always go as planned. When this happens, it's important that you persevere. Perseverance is the only way to get to your final goal, and it shows your ability to think on your feet as you reformulate your plan for success.

Can you remember a time when things didn't go as planned, and you had to make changes? How did those changes work out for you? Were you able to achieve your goal?

Do you work hard to earn money and save and budget the money you earn?

Many goals require money. You need to work to earn money and save and budget to ensure that you have the right amount of money when it's needed.

If you're currently working, do you work harder to earn more money when there's something you want to buy? Do you save the money you earn in case you need it later?

Do you use your education to achieve your goals and plan for your future?

Money isn't the only thing that makes plans possible; your education helps you formulate plans that are achievable and allows you to create efficient steps that get you closer to your end goal. For example, if you were building a storage chest, one of the steps to building the chest would be to measure the pieces of wood you want to use. Your education comes in handy here to ensure that you cut the right lengths of wood. As you complete the project, you may decide that you enjoyed building the chest so much that you want to pursue carpentry when you grow up.

Do you speak up and assert yourself when necessary?

As you plan for your future and set goals for yourself, you may encounter people who try to discourage you. It's important to be respectful and listen to what these people have to say, but it's also important to speak up and assert yourself when necessary. For example, if you share your goal with a friend and they tell you that

126

your goal is unattainable, speak up and assert yourself. Respectfully explain that you have thought everything through and already made a plan to achieve your goal.

Do you advocate for yourself and others?

Advocating for yourself is important, and advocating for others is as well. It's your responsibility to stand up and speak for those who cannot speak for themselves.

IMPROVE YOURSELF

You've been given a lot of advice in this book, more than you can ever put into practice at one time. You might feel overwhelmed by everything you've learned, but you're not meant to try every piece of advice immediately. The goal is to gradually improve your skills over time so that you'll have had practice in all areas by the time you're an adult.

Even as an adult, you won't have mastered these skills. Believe it or not, adults are still working on almost all the advice given here. This is because, as we mentioned in the growth mindset section of the book, there is always room for improvement. These skills don't have an end, which means you can get better no matter how good you already are. If you don't use these skills frequently, you can become rusty and out of practice, so even if you feel like you've got a good grasp on one skill or another, it's important to keep using it to keep it sharp.

Instead of trying to implement every piece of advice in this book at one time, try practicing one or two until you feel confident that you've improved in that area. Some skills can be practiced right away, like financial literacy, self-advocacy, setting goals, managing your time, and more.

Others will require a specific set of circumstances to practice. For example, it's difficult to practice learning from your mistakes until you make a mistake. But the good news is you can visualize what you will do the next time you make a mistake so that when that situation arises, you'll be prepared.

Visualization is a common technique that people use to create a mental picture of how a future event will go. Athletes use visualization all the time to help them score goals, shoot baskets, jump over hurdles, or perform any other aspect of their sport. The objective of visualization is to practice a skill in your mind so that you'll be more prepared when the actual event comes to pass.

Visualization allows you to imagine all the ways in which a situation might progress. For example, in Chapter 4, you learned how to talk to your friends and work out problems. However, maybe you don't have any problems with your friends right now. That's okay. You probably will have some conflict with them eventually, so think of a problem and imagine what your friend says and what you say back. How does that scenario end? What happens if your friend says or does something different? What do you say back, and how does that scenario end?

Visualization is one of the strongest practice techniques you can try to mentally prepare yourself for any situation. You may need a quiet space to visualize using your new skills, and sometimes, it helps to keep the room dark as well. That way, you're focusing only on practicing your new skills and not on anything distracting in the room.

Take all opportunities to practice the skills mentioned in this book when they present themselves in your life. Even if you feel uncomfortable at first, the more you practice these skills, the more comfortable you'll feel. Pretty soon, they'll just come naturally to you.

Keep Trying and Never Give Up

Not every skill in this book is going to be easy for you to learn. If they were, everyone would be experts in all of them. The key to learning these skills to the point where they can be useful in your life is to keep trying them even if you aren't successful at first. For example, you might try to save your money or stick to a budget, but then you see a new video game that looks so cool you dip into your savings and blow your budget to get it.

That's okay. It doesn't mean you're a failure at those skills. It just means that you need more practice when you try again. The next time a new video game comes out, you'll either have changed your budget to be able to afford it, or you'll remember how it felt to break your budget the last time, and you won't do it again. There's also the possibility that you'll fail again. It might take ten times before you get it right, and that's perfectly fine.

Whenever you're tempted to give up, there are some things you can do to ensure that you don't. First, remember *why* you're doing whatever it is you're doing. Are you saving money because you want to buy something that your parents won't buy for you? Are you trying to stick to a budget because you always have to ask your parents for more money before your allowance or paycheck comes in? Keeping the *why* at the forefront of your mind will help you keep going.

Second, be flexible. Sometimes, we get so set on meeting a goal by a certain date that when we mess up, we throw the entire plan in the trash. Things are going to happen along the way that you can't control, but you *can* control your response. Instead of getting frustrated that your plans changed, consider ways to get back on track as quickly as possible.

Finally, don't worry about what other people say. Your friends might try to get you to spend some of that money you're saving on things you don't want. They might say you're a kid, so you don't need to save money yet. That's their perspective, and they can do whatever is right for them. What's right for you, though, is what you want. Don't let other people's needs and wants derail you from achieving your goals. This is where your skills of self-advocacy and standing up for yourself will get a lot of practice.

Never giving up means keeping your eye on the prize. What is it that you want out of life that these skills can give you? Once you know that, it will be easier to remind yourself of your *why* and keep driving toward that prize.

Always Be Kind and Respectful

As you learn these new skills and put them to use in your life, it's important to remember that kindness and respect—toward yourself and others—go a long way toward becoming the type of person you want to be. Much of the advice given here is about valuing yourself, your thoughts, your opinions, your ideas, and your feelings. When you find value in yourself, you are being kind and respecting who you are.

Learning how to handle failure, managing your time better, keeping track of your money and spending, surrounding yourself with friends, staying positive, and taking care of yourself are all kind acts to yourself in different forms. For example, when you manage your time better, you're less stressed out when you have a deadline to meet, which means your body and mind don't have adverse reactions to stress.

Keeping track of your money and spending means you'll have money to do the kinds of things that make you feel good about yourself, which is a major part of self-care. Surrounding yourself with friends gives you a group of people who accept you for who you are, which increases your self-confidence and self-worth, both of which also increase your self-respect.

Being kind toward others is often easier than being kind to ourselves, but sometimes, we forget that others are dealing with issues just like we are, and we are less than kind. There's a saying that "everyone is fighting a battle we know nothing about," which means that even if someone's life looks easy, it probably isn't. It

131

doesn't cost a thing to be kind and respectful toward others, and you're more likely to get kindness and respect in return.

The best way to get an understanding of what someone is going through is to put yourself in their shoes. The more life experience you have, the easier it is to imagine what another person feels in their situation. For instance, right now, you might not know what it's like to try to teach a class that's noisy and won't settle down, but someday, you might be in front of a crowd that won't listen to what you have to say. Suddenly, you'll know how your teacher felt. The next time your teacher asks the class to quiet down, you'll be able to empathize and do what you can to make the classroom quieter.

For now, though, you can visualize how the other person might be feeling in an unfamiliar situation by imagining how you would feel. This takes a lot of self-reflection on your part, but you can make a positive difference in that person's life by imagining yourself in their shoes. Plus, you'll have improved your own skills as well.

Fun activity suggestion: Create a vision board with your goals and positive affirmations.

CONCLUSION

The life advice we give here is designed to give you a head start on becoming a more compassionate and overall happier adult. While we can't guarantee that you won't still have obstacles and challenges, these skills will allow you to more easily overcome them. Whether it's ensuring you have the right mindset, managing your time well, or coping with failure and disappointment, you'll have the opportunity to practice these skills over and over again throughout your life.

Not everyone gets the chance to learn these skills early, which makes it much harder for them when they have to learn them as adults. This is because consequences are often much harsher when you make mistakes as an adult than when you're a kid. This doesn't mean you won't have consequences when you mess up. It just means that because you're young, you have more of a safety net when you fall. That's why you're at the perfect age to begin learning these skills!

And don't let this book be the end of your learning. Becoming a lifelong learner is the key to continued personal growth and development. You can read much more about any of the topics we discuss here and even attend classes to help you hone your skills. There are also other activities you and your family can do together to practice these bits of advice so that you're ready when you face similar situations in your daily life.

Ask your family and friends to help you practice your new skills by roleplaying imagined scenarios or giving you real-world challenges that force you to use what you've learned in a practical way. For example, if you are working on budgeting money, have your parents give you a grocery budget for a week and take you to the grocery store to determine what you can buy while staying within your allotted amount of money.

To practice goal setting, think about the various careers you're interested in and set small goals leading up to that larger

134

achievement so that you can see what it's going to take to get there. If you want to practice self-advocacy, start small by asking your parents for minor privileges that you think you deserve. Remember that they might say no, but if you can deliver a convincing argument about why those privileges are important for you, it's not out of the question that they'll agree. Plus, it will give you experience in asking for what you need.

Use the internet to search for other types of activities and information related to the skills you want to develop. You aren't the first person who needs help in a specific area. Narrow your search to people in your age group so that you're presented with activities and suggestions that are appropriate for and accessible to you. You may need an adult's help with this, and that's okay. They are there to shape you into an adult and will be more than happy to assist.

One Step at a Time

As we explained at the very beginning of this book, no one is going to change overnight, and developing these skills takes a lot of practice and time. Work on one piece of advice at a time so that you don't become overwhelmed and frustrated. Choose one or two skills you want to work on first, then tackle the others in due time. In fact, situations will arise in the course of just living your life that will lend themselves to working on a particular skill.

However, you don't want to wait for those circumstances to arise before you get started. Pick one part of your life you want to improve and continue that improvement even when there are opportunities to put other skills into practice. As you'll discover, many of these skills are interrelated, which means you'll probably need more than one of them to conquer a challenge that comes your way.

When Will I Know I'm Done with This Book?

The short answer is that you'll never be done developing these skills. Adults continue to work on them throughout their entire lives, and you will too. Hopefully, the advice in this book will continue to be useful long after you've graduated from high school and moved into adulthood. That doesn't mean you have to take it with you to college or your first job, but if you ever need a reminder or a bit of advice, it's good to keep it around for reference.

Even if you feel like you've mastered one skill we've advised you to work on, there are probably others that you'll struggle with for longer. And that's perfectly fine. Some of this advice will come easily to you, while others will be more of a challenge. It's up to you to continue to improve the areas that you feel weakest in while still keeping your other skills strong.

Once you start developing these skill sets, you might discover that some of your friends need help with them as well. Sharing what you've learned will give them the same advantages. In turn, they can practice with you and you with them, which will only make everyone better.

Next Steps

After reading this book, it's time to put your new skills to the test. Try them out in real situations and assess your performance. Be as honest as possible to accurately understand what you improved and what you still need to work on. Ask yourself:

- What did I do best in this situation?
- What did I not do well in this situation?
- Did I achieve my goal? Why or why not?
- What do I want to do differently next time?
- What other advice in this book can I use to increase my odds of success?
- Who can I ask for help or advice?
- What else do I need to learn before this situation comes up again?
- Is there anything I can do right now to change the outcome?

To know if you're making progress on your development, talk with your family and teachers. Ask them to give you feedback on how you're doing. Feedback is critical to self-improvement. Even if you think you're doing well, there are always things you can refine. Outside observers are better at seeing those things than you are because we aren't always honest with ourselves, even if we want to be. Take their feedback into consideration and add it to what you already know about yourself to continue building your skills.

You've already taken a huge step by realizing you need to develop the skills mentioned in this book. Now you're ready to do the hard work of practicing them to get better and better with every use. By the time you're an adult, you'll have an edge over kids who waited to begin their self-improvement journey.

You're on the right path to living the life you want. It's time to try out your new skills and build your successes along the way.